The **foundations** of **learning**

The **foundations** of **learning**

EDITED BY
JULIE FISHER

Open University Press
Buckingham • Philadelphia

Open University Press
Celtic Court
22 Ballmoor
Buckingham
MK18 1XW

email: enquiries@openup.co.uk
world wide web: www.openup.co.uk

and
325 Chestnut Street
Philadelphia, PA 19106, USA

First Published 2002

A catalogue record of this book is available from the British Library

ISBN   0 335 20991 2 (pb)   0 335 20992 0 (hb)

Library of Congress Cataloging-in-Publication Data
The foundations of learning / [edited by] Julie Fisher.
     p. cm.
     Includes bibliographical references and index.
     ISBN 0-335-20992-0 — ISBN 0-335-20991-2 (pbk.)
     1. Early childhood education—Great Britain.   2. Learning.
     I. Fisher, Julie, 1950–

     LB1139.3.G7 F68 2002
     372.21′0941—dc21

                                                        2001050044

Typeset by Graphicraft Limited, Hong Kong
Printed in Great Britain by The Cromwell Press, Trowbridge

To Peter
and all the children in our lives

Contents

Notes on contributors

TONY BERTRAM
Dr Tony Bertram is Senior Research Fellow at University College Worcester, where he is Director of the Centre for Research in Early Childhood. He is Co-Director of the Effective Early Learning (EEL) Project and The Accounting Early for Life Long Learning (AcE) Project and is National Evaluator of the government's Early Excellence Centre Programme. He is President of the European Early Childhood Education Research Association and has recently worked as an early childhood review expert for the Organisation for Economic Co-operation and Development (OECD) on an international thematic review of early childhood education and care. He has published widely in the field of quality evaluation and development in early childhood, and the development of integrated services.

ADRIAN COOPER
As well as leading architectural projects with young children in schools, Adrian Cooper is a senior architect leading a team specializing in school designs in Oxfordshire.

MARION DOWLING
Marion Dowling is an early years specialist and a strong advocate for young children and those who work with them. During her career she has worked in playgroups, as a primary teacher and headteacher of a nursery school, in advisory posts in Suffolk and

Dorset and as one of Her Majesty's Inspectors of Schools. She is an Ofsted inspector and currently evaluator for two Early Excellence Centres. Marion has her own consultancy and runs training and professional development courses in this country and abroad. She is author of a number of books on early years, including *Education 3–5* and *Young Children's Personal, Social and Emotional Development*, published by Paul Chapman.

MARGARET EDGINGTON
Margaret Edgington is a freelance early years consultant offering a training and consultancy service, and campaigning and writing on early years issues. She has taught infant and nursery children in Lancashire, the Wirral and London and was headteacher of a new nursery school in inner London. Her experience includes educational home visiting, tutoring on a nursery nursing course, advisory teaching and work as a development officer at the National Children's Bureau. Her book *The Nursery Teacher in Action: Teaching 3, 4 and 5 year olds* was published in 1991 (2nd edition published 1998). She is an active member of the Early Years Curriculum Group (and has contributed to all its publications) and a Vice President of the National Campaign for Nursery Education. Her most recent work includes supporting the evaluation of two Early Excellence Centres.

JULIE FISHER
Julie Fisher is the Early Years Adviser for Oxfordshire. Before moving to Oxfordshire she was lecturer in Early Childhood Education at the University of Reading. She has been headteacher of two schools – one an infant and nursery school in outer London, the other a nursery, first and middle combined school in Buckinghamshire. Julie is Chair of the Early Years Curriculum Group and is the early years representative on the national executive of the National Association of Inspectors, Advisers and Consultants. Representing these bodies she sits on the Early Childhood Education Forum and the Qualifications and Curriculum Authority's Early Years Focus Group. Julie is author of a number of articles on early education as well as her book *'Starting from the Child?'*

CHRISTINE PASCAL
Professor Christine Pascal currently holds the Chair of Early Childhood Education at University College Worcester, where she is Director of the Centre for Research in Early Childhood. She is Co-Director of the Effective Early Learning (EEL) Project and The

Accounting Early for Life Long Learning (AcE) Project and is National Evaluator of the Government's Early Excellence Centre Programme. She is also currently Specialist Adviser to the House of Commons Select Committee Inquiry on Early Years and is a member of the DfEE Foundation Stage Working Group. She co-founded the European Early Childhood Education Research Association and works extensively across Europe in her early childhood research and development work. She has written widely on the subject of quality early childhood education and is committed to developing integrated services for all children and their families.

LINDA POUND
Linda Pound has, throughout her long career, worked in many sectors and phases of education. Her current role at the University of North London is as Academic Leader for Early Childhood Programmes, which allows her to continue to promote the quality of provision for young children and their families. Prior to this Linda was Primary Inspector with responsibility for early years in the London Borough of Greenwich. She is an active member of the Early Years Curriculum Group and represents them at the Early Childhood Education Forum.

GILLIAN PUGH OBE
Dr Gillian Pugh has been Chief Executive of Coram Family since 1997. She was previously at the National Children's Bureau, most recently as director of the Early Childhood Unit. While in this post she set up and chaired the Early Childhood Education Forum from 1993–97. Over the past 20 years Gillian has advised governments in the UK and overseas on the development of policy for young children, on coordination of services, on curriculum, on parental involvement, and on parent education and support. She has published over 30 books including *Contemporary Issues in the Early Years* (three editions); *Confident Parents, Confident Children; Preventative Work with Families* and *Training to Work in the Early Years*. She was a member of the Rumbold Committee on the education of children of 3 to 5 (DES 1990), of the RSA Start Right enquiry (Ball 1994) and the Audit Commission study of early education (1996).

WENDY SCOTT
Wendy Scott has been involved in teaching, lecturing, inspecting, supporting and developing early years provision and practice over many years. She is ever more convinced of the importance

of enabling children, families and communities to establish firm foundations for learning and living together, and is continuing to learn herself as a specialist adviser to the Department for Education and Skills. Prior to this role she was Chief Executive of the British Association for Early Childhood Education. Wendy writes here in a personal capacity and does not necessarily reflect government policy.

PAULINE TRUDELL
Pauline Trudell taught for many years in inner London nursery schools and classes. She has worked as an advisory teacher and as a lecturer in education and Course Tutor for the Early Childhood Studies Scheme at the University of North London. She is presently Head of Portman Early Childhood Centre in Westminster.

Acknowledgements

This book is the result of many people's dedication and commitment to early years. My first tribute is to Lesley Staggs who, as Principal Manager at QCA, steered the Foundation Stage through its many delicate developmental stages and brought it to fruition. Second, my thanks and admiration go to Wendy Scott. As Chief Executive of the British Association for Early Childhood Education, Wendy invited me to speak at a conference* and suggested *The Foundations of Learning* as a working title! That conference talk, and this book, would not have been written without the imagination and inspiration of Adrian Cooper. His professional expertise has ensured the architectural references throughout this text are robust and his enthusiasm for the project enabled my initial tentative ideas to flourish. My grateful thanks go to all the contributors, each one a specialist in the field of early childhood and each with a demanding full-time job to do! Yet every one has risen to the challenge of their chapter, inspired by the possibilities that the Foundation Stage has brought

---

* Many of the ideas in this book came from those in my presentation at the BAECE Conference 'Principles, Processes and Goals for Early Learning' held in London on 22 January 2000, which was published subsequently as an article in *Early Education* in summer 2000. I am grateful to all those at BAECE for their willingness to let me extend these ideas still further.

about and prepared to reflect on what it means for them and their work. I am very grateful to Shona Mullen at Open University Press who had the vision to commission this book and to see its potential, and to Anita West who steered me patiently through the complexities of being an editor. I have been overwhelmed by all those who have heard or read about the foundations metaphor and contacted me about it, offering fresh insights and ideas and extending my own thinking. Finally, my loving thanks go again to David. By the time this book is published we will have moved house, and have new foundations of our own.

Introduction: the importance of firm foundations . . . an analogy with architecture

☐ ADRIAN COOPER

In the year of the new millennium, the UK government introduced the Foundation Stage of learning as a distinct phase of educational experience for children from age 3 to the end of the reception year (QCA 2000). I know this because I met an early education specialist called Julie Fisher! As early years adviser in Oxfordshire, it was Julie's task to brief the architects working for the local authority on the principles behind this new educational initiative and explain the implications it would have for children's learning and the environments in which that learning would take place.

The choice of the word 'foundation' to represent this stage of learning was obviously a carefully selected metaphor, intended to emphasize that, upon this stage, all future achievement and attainment depends. As an architect I couldn't help but be intrigued by the analogy between the foundations of learning and the foundations of buildings. Julie and I struck up a dialogue to establish how and in what ways the similarities of the principles underpinning our two separate professions might have much in common.

As we talked, Julie and I discovered seven facts about the foundations of buildings which held resonance for the foundations of learning. In this book, the seven facts are explored by seven experts in the field of early education. What is powerful is that, for all of their distinctiveness, each chapter returns to the crucial importance of children's early learning. More particularly, the chapters reinforce and redefine that the best learning opportunities are those that give children the space, time and support to be independent and effective learners. The right space, time and support are all critical elements of effective foundations in architecture, and appropriate and adequate investment in all three is vital.

As an architect, I represent the 'jack of all trades' in the construction industry. I need to understand the broad implications on the whole process of all disciplines of design and construction. What inspires architects is the inseparable link between architecture and society. Archaeologists scrutinize the unearthed remains of ancient living quarters to deduce early social patterns. The late twentieth-century urban patterns of cul-de-sacs, for example, speak volumes about the attitudes of the day. By design, architects can help to determine the society by the quality or propriety of their architecture. In the same way, I am pleased to play my small vicarious part in this debate on education, confident that the debate will yield significant social benefit.

Funny or uncanny, there is a serious point to the examination of the 'foundations' metaphor. First, it lends a refreshing objectivity to the arguments for high-quality early years provision – many of which, I understand, are not new to teachers and other educators. But to stand back and contemplate how the metaphors parallel each other certainly served well to introduce my untrained mind to the issues at stake in early care and education. Second, the facts which I outline about architectural foundations are true – not glib gimmicks or anecdotes. There is hard evidence to support the assertion that the right foundations – in both our fields – are crucial.

Fact 1: Foundations take longer to create than buildings

Taking into account the design as well as the construction, foundations take longer to create than buildings. Architects have to look at the site, locality and the physical environment of their location before they can set about making the necessary detailed and extensive calculations upon which designs are drawn up. Whatever kind of building is to be constructed, the principles about laying good foundations apply.

People are often surprised about how long the design process takes. The construction of a brand new primary school will take about twelve months. For an architect, this is the easy bit. Advising on site acquisition, negotiating planning benefit, gaining planning approval, Building Regulations approval, establishing leases, Rights of Way and determining the services availability on site (electricity, gas, water, telecomms . . .) and detailed soil investigations with specialists can easily add up to three or four years' work before a 'sod is turned'.

This advance preparation and research is paramount to the success of the project. Woe betide a project hitting site without all the parameters understood. Disaster awaits a construction which digs foundations before resolution of the building characteristics. Disaster or serious compromise. You cannot build a three-storey house on the foundations meant for two storeys. Nor a skyscraper on the foundations of a petrol station.

Fact 2: The higher the building, the firmer the foundations have to be

Building regulations require architects and engineers to put in double the strength of foundations than is actually necessary. All foundations have a margin of safety built into them. Particularly tall buildings are subject to additional pressure from the elements. The higher you want a building to reach the greater must be the margin of safety and the stronger the foundations.

As with a tree whose roots below ground typically mirror its canopy in spread and sometimes depth, tall buildings depend for their stability on deep foundations. Depth in foundations equates to scientific investigation. The bearing capacity of the sub-strata, the water table, the consistency of the soils and the proximity of faults in strata need to be rigorously calculated by engineers to ensure the superstructure is firmly rooted.

Architects can be frustrating people to work with. Most engineers will attest to this. Architects do not shun complexity – they are innate problem solvers using their training and imagination to juggle competing priorities. An architect will typically withhold decision making as long as possible to ensure the several priorities of a brief have each been addressed and slotted into an appropriate hierarchy. You cannot rush this process. Simplification or generalization ultimately constrain this design process and compromise the result. Too early a fix upon a solution or desired outcome preordains the limits of a building's success. For example, a building is unlikely to offer wheelchair friendly access throughout if this is not considered at some stage of the design. Design is meticulous, all-embracing, unhurried and expensive in personpower.

This initial maelstrom of conflicting design criteria, this complex mess of priorities, may well resolve into an elegantly simple design. Conversely, a design based upon a simplified list of criteria will always be a skeletal compromise.

Fact 3: The more stress a building is likely to face, the more flexible the foundations need to be

When it is known that a building will come under strain then it is necessary for the structure of its foundations to be flexible. Even in the UK, certain areas are rated quite highly as potential earthquake zones, and the foundations of buildings in those areas must be designed to take the prospective strain. In such areas, architects and engineers will use steel frameworks for the foundations rather than the concrete frameworks which are too rigid. If foundations are too rigid then ultimately they will not support the construction above.

Once built upon, the foundations will need to resist loadings imposed upon them transferred through the superstructure of the building into the ground. Therefore, foundation design needs also to anticipate 'live' pressures on the building during its life and changes which may occur. Foundations may need to transfer the superstructure windloads, seismic activity, bomb blast, future building extensions or changes to building use. Flexible frameworks in the superstructure mean that earthquakes are likely to wreak havoc in the building. A rigid building is shaken into destruction by seismic tremors. Weaker windows than structure will mean that a blast from an explosion will not affect the structure of the building and therefore prevent collapse. Building adaptability needs to be built in from the foundations upward.

Anticipating an evolving future is part of an architect's or engineer's brief. Ensuring that a building will cope in extraordinary circumstances is vital. Of course, failure to allow the building to flex in response to these pressures will greatly reduce the project's effectiveness when the worst scenario strikes. Anticipating a diverse range of stresses in the design stages guarantees a building a long and fruitful existence, despite whatever fate might deal.

Fact 4: When building on poor ground, the foundations must be strengthened to compensate

The best foundation is permanent, secure rock. The worst is shifting sands. If an architect builds on unstable ground, the advance preparation for foundations takes longer. All calculations need to compensate for poor ground and such calculations take considerable time and expertise. On problematic ground, architects may need to draw on the expert help of a structural engineer. Poor ground does not mean that you cannot build. With the right investment of time, expertise and money, even the poorest foundations can be made to be stable and secure in the end.

Every building is a prototype. Even prefabricated classrooms manufactured on production lines need tailored foundations to suit the particular spot they will occupy. Standard details which apply universally do not exist. Instead, each design is unique and specialist advice is required to expose the nuances of every application. Foundations in sand differ from those in clay, and from those on rock, or wet shale, or near trees or burst water mains. Nearly every situation will yield an appropriate foundation design and permit building, given the correct specialist advice and the necessary investment.

Specialism in the building industry is rife. Some architects' practices specialize exclusively in hospitals. An employer respects this experience. A practice without this experience is unlikely to be offered the commission to build a hospital. A bricklayer will not be asked to carve timber stairs. Expert understanding is treasured and crucial to ensuring propriety of the design purpose. If an engineer is needed who is experienced in calculating the reinforcement required to strengthen concrete in a dam then informed advice from that source is superior to a steel framing specialist. Ill-informed design is worthless and likely to fail. A thorough understanding of the context of a foundation design is indispensable for a construction company with a reliable future. With the right specialist advice, anything is possible.

Fact 5: If new buildings are to be added to existing buildings, making the right connections between the foundations is crucial

When a new building is added to an existing building, the connections must be very well engineered. If the wrong connections are made, it can destroy not only the new building but the existing building as well. Appropriate connections allow the new building to settle and find its own level independently and without being forced or constrained. The more considered the connections are, the more likely it is for the whole building to end up more robust and adaptive to its environment.

As Codes of Practice used in foundation designs have evolved over the years, as construction techniques improve, as research yields deeper insight into the performance of different materials, it is rarely possible to determine the criteria used to design a foundation for an existing building. When extending such an existing building to give new life, a changed purpose or larger population, it is dangerous to make simple assumptions about the existing design. New buildings often divorce their structure from the existing so as to disturb it the least. The connections between the old and the new buildings are very carefully considered – often incorporating slip joints to allow differential settlement. An analogy with town planning applies. New buildings, attracting different people, different traffic, different microclimate and different rateable values are usually permitted on the grounds that the new building is compatible with the future of the locality, enriching the community, bringing new employment. Planners and architects study the impact of new uses on towns and cities and how individual buildings work. Some additions are undesirable, others not. In each instance the impact needs to be assessed. Attention needs to be paid to the interactions of new and old so as to understand fully and therefore promote environmental or social improvement. If the interactions are misjudged, or studies omitted, additions to the townscape will not function fully in the broader built environment.

Fact 6: When testing foundations, early strength is not a reliable predictor of later strength

Every time you pour concrete you have to test its strength. The concrete is poured into cubes and sent for analysis. The concrete is tested after seven days and again after 28 days. If it fails the seven-day test, the architect does not go back to the builder and say start again. First, it is possible for the concrete to pass the seven-day test and then fail later on. Equally, it is possible for the concrete to fail the seven-day test and then pass later on. So, concrete's overall strength is not accurately determined by early testing.

There is a complicated chemical reaction taking place as concrete 'cures'. The cement reacts with water exothermically – giving off heat. The water is either given off as vapour or chemically combined within the reaction. Achieving the right proportions in the mix is very important. As time progresses, the water proportion diminishes and the concrete strength increases – measured at intervals to check the early strength of the concrete. The proportion of water depends upon ambient temperature, relative humidity, salt content and aggregate density. Thus the reaction takes place at a varying, non-linear rate. Therefore, although interim tests give a clue to ultimate strength, they are not wholly reliable in predicting later strength.

Similarly, in the design process, as a design matures, more corrections are made to accommodate further design criteria. Early simplified testing of the design skews the results toward an always incomplete set of standards. Such results could easily corrupt the design development. Instead, there has to be acknowledgement in any testing that a whole raft of design criteria will have an impact. The healthiest design development will be one where the designer is constantly bombarded with stimuli seeking inquiry and resolution.

Fact 7: If foundations are inadequate, it is very, very expensive to underpin them later on

Remedial work entails exposing and underpinning foundations in order for them to be adequate. Every building changes over time. It reacts to temperature, environmental conditions, external and internal pressures. Good foundation laying anticipates this with expansion joints which allow different parts of the building to flex. Architects know that if a building is put under undue or unexpected stress, it is very difficult at that point to shore up the foundations. Equally, buildings that are likely to require a variety of uses need foundations that can respond to the likely changes.

If foundations are inadequately prepared, planned, designed, poured or cured, a weakness in their future fitness for purpose is cast in concrete. This may never be exposed. However, much as back trouble can all but disable a sufferer completely, such a residual flaw is likely to seriously compromise future development. If the development is already built when the flaw is discovered, rebuilding or modifying the foundations can be catastrophic in terms of expense, time and building welfare.

The sooner a flaw is rectified, the less costly the implications. At the design stage, the only cost will be time to redesign and the costs of redesign. If discovered at pouring of foundation stage, the cost of demolition will need to be added, together with increased re-excavation and redesign time. If the foundations are built upon by the time of the discovery, the cost is magnified by the increased demolition costs, full redesign, building downtime (when a contractor is unable to proceed with their work) . . . It is a common epithet in an architect's drawing office that there rarely seems time to do the job right first time, but you always seem to make time to do the design again if necessary.

Conclusion

Review of the arguments in the book leads to a conclusion that there is no substitute for heeding professional evidence and expertise, for allowing time to get things right, for appropriate financial investment. This might require a review of current educational impetus. Generalization to create consistency is doubly flawed. Instead, the correct application of the principles of good foundation design might allow a focus on individual needs rather than general ones, on a broader definition of richness in children's education and more on a quality process than on creating a narrowly defined product.

ONE

Breadth and depth in early foundations

☐ **LINDA POUND**

Introduction

The introduction of the Foundation Stage has provided an opportunity to rethink or re-evaluate the ways in which we educate young children. In the recent past the pressures placed upon schools to perform well in league tables have led some policy makers at local and national level to believe misguidedly that an earlier start to formal learning will ensure a better result by 11 years of age. In many areas of education the assertion that children must reach a certain point or stage by a particular age has created an assumption that decisions can be taken about where children must begin. Teachers in reception classes in particular may feel compelled to attempt to overlay children's current understandings, especially those about written language and number, with the prescribed teaching set out in the literacy and numeracy strategies, or in the school's own long-term curriculum plans. In this way, it is not foundations of learning that are set down – rather what already exists in the child's mind is generally isolated from that which is taught in school. This overlay of information – if it is not embedded in and connected to what the child already knows – will not result in independent, reflective and adaptive learning (Pound 2000). The fact that the curriculum can be parcelled up into nice, neat, teachable packages does not mean that that is how it is most effectively learnt.

The opportunity afforded by the introduction of the Foundation Stage to review curriculum and pedagogy in the early years has been welcomed by early childhood practitioners since it has provided a platform for voicing and exploring the ever-deepening understanding that we have of young children's learning. That understanding will never be complete, since the human brain is essentially adaptive and dynamic, but new technological advances are giving us increasing insight into the processes of learning. One exciting feature of these advances is that the 'new' findings so often serve to reinforce the understanding which skilled early years practitioners have developed over generations.

The foundations of buildings, like human learning, are complex and largely hidden. The enthralling thing about working with young children is that in the period in which the foundations are being laid for what has to be a lifelong process of change and adaptation much of their learning appears to be visible. We watch their play and understand something of their thinking. We might spot schemas, we might determine patterns in their activity and as speech emerges we are privileged to hear their externalized thoughts developing. As they grow older, they internalize increasing amounts of language (Vygotsky 1976) and learn to mask feelings and ideas, weighing up their effects on others. But in the early years there is a refreshing openness. When a 3-year-old asks why you've got creases on your face, why you've got black things on your teeth or if you're going to die soon, you know there is no malice intended. They are simply trying to understand their world, to lay foundations for the edifices which they will build in the future.

Like the viewing platforms created on building sites, when we work with young children we are often enabled to see the foundations being laid out. Children's play, their questions and explanations are a way of standing on the viewing platform. As the days go by, and the structure is created, the foundations become less and less visible. Not being able to see them does not make them of less importance. Indeed, as the structure grows, the foundations become increasingly important if the building is not to collapse or slide into the ground.

If we are able to observe young children with an open mind and a respectful eye, we can gain an insight into the ways in which they are thinking and the connections they are making as their thinking and reasoning develop. Vivian Gussin Paley has a wonderful capacity to observe the detail of children's thinking. She does this by engaging her class in a curriculum based around the telling of the children's stories (which are dictated to an adult) and the acting out of the stories each day. This storytelling/story-acting approach gives adults and children a window on thinking (their own and others'), a way of reflecting on the foundations of their lifelong learning abilities. Paley writes (1981: 4):

> You can . . . write a book about thinking – by recording the conversations, stories, and playacting that take place as events and problems are encountered. A wide variety of thinking emerges, as morality, science, and society share the stage with fantasy. If magical thinking seems most conspicuous, it is because it is the common footpath from which new trails are explored. I have learned not to resist this magic but to seek it out as a legitimate part of 'real' school.

Gardens or buildings

In using building foundations as an analogy for the foundations of young children's learning, we should not forget the other major metaphor that has been widely used. The notion of the blossoming of the child's intellect and personality, their unfolding like a leaf or flower has long lain behind the philosophy of early childhood education. Just as in the buildings and classrooms of Reggio Emilia the underlying philosophy of Malaguzzi (1993), with its emphasis on reflection, is symbolized by the widespread use of light, glass and mirrors, so the metaphor of the garden was for a long time the dominant theme in provision for young children, particularly in the English nursery school, many of which were established in the first half of the twentieth century.

The most famous manifestation of the nursery garden is probably the Rachel McMillan Nursery School in Deptford where classrooms are still known as shelters. The school began as a night camp for children at risk of TB and other infection in 1911. Lowndes (1960: 76) cites Margaret McMillan describing the importance she placed on fresh air:

> The new nursery schools must be in the open air. There must, of course, be shelter and heating and common sense. But men must learn to build for the open air . . . The idea at the back of the builder of yesterday was shelter – a shelter from animals, foes, weather. But the child's worst foes today are germs. All the rest is as nothing in view of that danger.

From a very different starting point Chelsea Open Air Nursery School was opened in 1929 in order to provide challenge for over-privileged children, whom the benefactor claimed were crippled by not being allowed to take risks. These two schools offer an excellent example of the many ways in which the judgements made by insightful practitioners in the past is increasingly being supported by current research.

The *Curriculum Guidance for the Foundation Stage* (QCA 2000) has been instrumental in halting a trend which has been emerging over many years. In including a requirement to plan rich and stimulating experiences indoors and out, staff in settings which have not placed much emphasis on the outdoor classroom are having to rethink their practice. The guidance gives as the rationale for outdoor provision the notion that 'children are enabled to learn by working on a larger, more active scale than is possible indoors' (QCA 2000: 15). There are, however, many additional reasons why outdoor provision is essential to the foundation stage. Children's worst enemies today are not the germs, in fact some scientists suggest that lack of germs is harming children's immune systems. There are however the ever-present foes of mental stress (Mental Health Foundation 1999) and a lack of opportunity to take risks and assert independence (Furedi 2001). Learning does not occur where there is stress, nor does it occur without some errors and risk.

There is no intention to replace the metaphor of the garden with one of a building. The importance of being outdoors, in the fresh air, with space to run, time to play and the opportunity to experience those phenomena which can only be experienced outdoors – rain, sunshine, wind and trees – will always remain an essential ingredient in creating firm foundations for lifelong learning and personal development – not just in the earliest years.

The final point to be made about the central analogy of this book is about who is the builder. This is not an easy question to answer. Current research about the brain tells us that each of us is the builder of our own brain (see for example Gopnik, Meltzoff and Kuhl 1999) and, therefore, as suggested above, the child is the builder. However, learning does not occur without social contact – and what role does that leave for the adults who work with children: are they the site managers, architects, or perhaps the ones who grant planning permission? These are questions to ponder on as you read and questions which are central to the current debates about young children's learning. The fact that adults do not control children's minds or seek to predetermine what is learnt does not mean that they are not active in the process.

The following sections will refer to design elements, site, locality and physical environment. Children's thinking and learning has foundations which are not predetermined but which have to be created from a blueprint, common to all humans.

The design of human minds

The blueprint for human learning has taken millennia to create. Over long periods human brains have evolved to deal with the changing contexts which we ourselves have created. The essence of the human brain is its flexibility. Fifty or even twenty years ago the changes which we face on a day-to-day basis could not have been guessed at. Fortunately our brains have been designed to cope with this. We lay foundations in our minds for buildings of unknown shapes and for unforeseen functions. Reflex actions are of relatively little importance in humans – because they are designed for speedy, unthinking response, not considered flexible action. Our long years of infant dependency have evolved in order to allow us to spend years playing, discovering and exploring so that we can be inventive throughout our lives. The way in which the brain has evolved continues to determine learning throughout our lives – in ways which we, with the help of neuroscientists, are only just beginning to understand. Plasticity and resilience are what is needed for thinking and problem solving in the ever-changing contexts which humans create and inhabit. With the right foundations human brains can go on adapting and changing.

Movement has always played an important part in development and learning. Susan Greenfield (1997) goes so far as to say that if we didn't move we wouldn't need a brain. While important to us all, movement plays a vital function in young children's learning and is responsible for bridging learning in the two hemispheres of the brain. Movement, practised over time and in a playful fashion, creates patterns in the brain and networks which span and combine logical thought with emotional thinking.

Evolutionary psychologist Steven Mithen (1996) hypothesizes very convincingly about the way in which human brain plasticity and adaptability has developed throughout our evolution. He suggests that it is the interactional language which parents and carers use when establishing contact with their babies which has enabled humans to use all areas of the brain together, rather than in isolation, as other species do. Social language created 'cognitive fluidity' (Mithen 1996: 184) and this enabled humans to represent, for example, technical and natural history intelligences in language, allowing ideas to move across areas of the brain.

Language which has been so instrumental in establishing the blueprint of human thinking has a very long history. Storr (1992: 12) puts forward theories which underline a widespread belief (proposed by Blacking 1987) that 'singing and dancing preceded the development of verbal interchange' by several hundred thousand years. He even suggests that dance preceded walking. Storr (1992: 12) quotes from Cranston (1983: 289): 'Primitive men [*sic*] sing to one another in order to express their feelings before they come to speak to one another in order to express their thoughts.' Storr, citing a number of fascinating sources, further suggests that early language was chanted, and that language may have been drawn from an ancient poem or ritualistic form of language.

This sequence is mirrored in young children's development. Babies undoubtedly dance before they walk; just watch their rhythmic jiggling whenever they hear bouncy music or their bodily engagement in familiar rhymes or songs – whole sections of their bodies from their toes to their eyebrows moving in time. They also sing (or at least use musical elements) long before they speak. Children's earliest attempts at communicative utterance focus on pitch and intonation. In their earliest days they rehearse the 'tunes' which we use in our everyday language, and adults encourage them in this. Karmiloff-Smith (1994: 40) quotes from a parent describing this phenomenon quite vividly:

> I keep trying to speak to her normally – but it's odd, I find myself quite naturally talking in a sing-song voice whenever I'm with her. When one of my friends is here, I try to talk normally. You feel such an idiot. Somehow it just comes out, like there was a special language for babies that we never have to learn. I've noticed people in the street do it too. The newsagent does it the most – a real piece of opera whenever he sees Evelyn.

There are other aspects of our linguistic and therefore cognitive past which are important aspects of our embedded design as learners and which continue to be an important part in the foundations of our thinking. In his book *Primary Understanding*, Egan (1988) describes the importance of rhythm, rhyme, narrative, metaphor and metre in the development of thinking. Egan describes these tools for thinking as being the remnant of our oral past. Metaphor or symbolic understanding is an important feature of our cognitive design. The value of story in developing thinking, or laying foundations for later learning, is widely acknowledged. Paley (1991: 163) asks why fairy stories are so ubiquitous when the children's own stories are their intuitive way of interpreting or representing their world and experiences. She writes:

> Putting aside the fact that fairy tales cannot be avoided, why are they needed? Perhaps because they are such good stories. They represent the adult version of childhood fantasy, presented in a cohesive, theatrical style that is perfectly suited to the endemic thinking of children. Not the least of the fairy tale's superior power lies in its obvious connection to mankind's fantasies as represented in the play of young children.

Fromm (1951) held a similar view. In his work as a psychoanalyst, he focuses on myths and believes that our dreams are born of the same symbolic language, *The Forgotten Language*, as he entitles his book. He claims that the myths of all ancient civilizations are written in this forgotten language, which we only reclaim in our dreams. He writes:

> Symbolic language is a language in which inner experiences, feelings and thoughts are expressed as if they were sensory experiences, events in the outer world . . . It is the one universal language the human race has even developed, the same for all cultures and throughout history. It is a language with its own grammar and syntax, as it were, a language one must understand if one is to understand the meaning of myths, fairy tales and dreams.
>
> (Fromm 1951: 7)

Playfulness is another crucial element of creating the foundations of learning – found in music, dance, tool creation and imagination. Papousek (1994) underlines the importance of play. He claims that since playfulness (like music) is present in all human behaviour it must have an evolutionary purpose. He maps out the ways in which human play including music can be seen as arising from and building on the play and music of other species and genera. Drawing on this knowledge, the function of music in the human blueprint is, suggests Papousek, to make it possible to communicate in situations where communication would otherwise be difficult. Music allows us to open up communication with young babies. It allows us to express feelings of joy, love, sorrow and grief that might be difficult to put into words. Music enables us to express social cohesion – in church, the school hall and on the football pitch. It is used by adults to represent emotions to babies (Fernald 1993) and at a later stage, at around five to six months, to familiarize young children with the segmentation of spoken language. Playful rhymes like 'Walking round the garden' and 'This little piggy went to market' serve this purpose and have their parallels in other languages. Response to music feeds our learning and development throughout life. It is the last capacity to be lost in dementia, as the brain declines (Storr 1992).

Play allows children to represent ideas, to rehearse and practise and to explore relationships, materials, objects, ideas and feelings. It is play which creates in the brain the neural networks which will serve as a foundation for learning throughout life. It is closely linked to imagination and to creativity and it is playing with ideas which allows humans to understand humour and create jokes. Playfulness and imaginative response are what have marked out humans from other species and it is these very playful responses which promote learning – not just in infancy but throughout life. Claxton (1997) cites an interesting study in which adult subjects were invited to play at being airline pilots. In preparation for the simulated flight they were given an eye test. Later, as part of the role play, they were required to read material which was comparable to that which had been used in the eye test. Claxton (1997: 126) writes:

> It was found that the vision of nearly half of the 'pilots' had improved significantly. Other groups of subjects, who were not immersed in the role, showed no such improvement. By changing the sense of self, more precise information can become available to consciousness.

Many of the design features of human learning are embedded deep within the brain, in the limbic system which controls emotion and memory. It is no accident that the tools for learning which humans have developed serve both these functions. Many of the things which we do not consciously remember continue to shape our responses throughout life (Siegel 1999). Important aspects of learning such as motivation and self-confidence are based on forgotten or hidden experiences. In order to have been learnt these experiences were oft-repeated – slowly learnt and slow to be forgotten.

Taking account of the site for lifelong learning: the human brain

The earliest foundations for learning occur before birth. The design of human brains and bodies is exceedingly complex. The recent publication of the genome map was greeted with some disbelief. Many scientists had expected a far larger number of genes to be identified. The fact that the number finally determined was smaller than expected further suggests that the human mind is not as predetermined as some would want to believe. This view is reinforced by neuroscience. Although the evidence from brain studies frequently relies on animal studies and therefore cannot be interpreted in human terms without a great deal of caution (Bruer 2000) it undoubtedly has something to tell us about the design of human learning. Gopnik *et al.* (1999: 182) suggest that:

> The new scientific research doesn't say that parents should provide special 'enriching' experiences to children over and above what they experience in everyday life. It does suggest though, that a radically deprived environment could cause damage . . . This early research . . . established an important point – a brain can physically expand and contract and change depending on experience.

What brain studies further reveal is what complex foundations for learning humans have. Throughout the years of the Foundation Stage (and well beyond) children's brains are twice as active as those of adults (Gopnik *et al.* 1999). By the age of 2 their brains weigh 70 per cent of those of adults and by 6 years of age 90 per cent (Talay-Ongan 1998). Human brains have often been likened to computers but in fact they are far more complex and adaptable. Experience of every kind influences the way in which the brain develops and babies are able to combine information from their senses and feelings to gain additional understandings. The relationship between feelings and learning has been well documented by LeDoux (1999) and is daily experienced by us all. The link between the senses is particularly pronounced in young children and they rely on the combination of information that comes to them often unconsciously through all kinds of sensations (Donaldson 1993).

Humans are born with a wide and surprising range of competencies. At birth babies recognize human faces as being like their own and can imitate facial expressions (Gopnik *et al.* 1999). The authors suggest that this has been learnt kinaesthetically – that with our tongues, for example, we have come to know what our own faces look like. In the womb we have also learnt to recognize familiar tunes, languages and voices and shortly after birth demonstrate preferences for the familiar.

Newborns can also distinguish between two and three objects (Dahaene 1997) and in their earliest months can match two or three drumbeats with two or three objects. Dehaene further reports that 'as early as four days of age, a baby can decompose speech sounds into smaller units – syllables – that it can then enumerate' (1997: 51). Moreover they are able to recognize when mistakes have been made in the addition and subtraction of numbers up to three. In an experiment described by Karmiloff-Smith (1994), Mickey Mouse dolls were used with five-month-old babies. When shown actions which involved the apparent removal of a doll from a small group, or addition to it, the babies registered surprise when the number finally revealed differed from that which might have been expected.

We don't know whether this remarkable numerical ability is what Ramachandran and Blakeslee (1999: 265) have called *hardwired* (and therefore part of our evolving brain design) or whether it can be attributed to our propensity to seek out rules. They write:

> Our ability to engage in numerical computations . . . seems so effortless that it's easy to jump to the conclusion that it is 'hard-wired'. But, in fact, it *became* effortless only after the introduction of two basic concepts – place value and zero – in India during the third century AD.

There is undoubtedly a complex relationship between nature and nurture. A similar conundrum exists in relation to language learning. While some place emphasis on Chomsky's hypothesis (1957) that humans possess a hard-wired Language Acquisition Device (LAD), others stress the propensities that babies are born with – to interact socially and to seek out rules – as the crucial factor in laying the foundations for future learning. Bruner (1983a) emphasizes the first of these factors, describing mothers [*sic*] as Language Acquisition Support Systems (LASS). There is no doubt that these supportive qualities apply equally to other carers. Indeed we know that even very young children, under the age of 3, use the same supportive strategies when attempting to interact with babies (Dunn 1988).

Newborn babies have other surprising abilities. Donaldson (1993) describes a variety of experiments with very young babies in which through various mechanisms they are given the means to operate mobiles, work out increasingly complicated switching devices, focus pictures. In short the studies demonstrate that within their first six months of life, babies 'can quickly learn to exercise effective control. What is more, they seem pleased when they do so' (Donaldson 1993: 34). She concludes that such pleasure in exercising control implies knowledge of a world to be controlled and a sense of self as a controlling agent.

This desire to control the world is underlined by the human ability to represent ideas and experiences. Outward manifestations of this emerge early in their second year of life as babies begin to be aware of the way in which one object can be made to stand for another – this block can be a car, this box a mobile phone. Symbols representing significant people in their lives help young children to keep those people in mind. A bit of mummy's nightdress, wrapped around the thumb and held closely to the nose, helps the child to remember that person who is no longer visible and to be reassured that she will reappear.

The ability to symbolize (and to represent in story and imagination) is connected to babies' remarkable problem-solving abilities. At a very young age they can bring knowledge gained from one situation to bear in another (Karmiloff-Smith 1994; Gopnik *et al.* 1999), and symbols or tools for thinking enable us to do this. One of the experiments described (Gopnik *et al.* 1999) involved three-month-old babies being connected to a mobile by a ribbon tied to their ankles. If they are presented with the same mobile a week later, they immediately kick the same foot – with or without a ribbon tied to it. However if it is a different mobile they won't kick. Although they are making some clear connections in order to solve problems, babies seem much less clear about what is actually solving the problem. At the same time as kicking they coo and gurgle at the mobile as though coaxing it or using their human problem-solving abilities.

Piaget (1952), whose work predates studies of this sort, understood the incomplete nature of children's thinking but promoted respect for it by emphasizing the logic, by reminding us that it is based on the limited nature of their experience. They, like all of us, base their guesses or theories on what they have experienced. In his work, Piaget placed an emphasis on logical thought as the basis of problem solving and learning. Gardner, uncomfortable with problem solving, learning or cognition being thought of solely or primarily in scientific terms, reviewed the notion of cognition. He writes (Gardner 1999: 28):

> When I began to think of what it meant to be 'developed', when I asked myself what optimal human development is, I became convinced that developmentalists had to pay much more attention to the skills and capacities of painters, writers, musicians, dancers, and other artists. Stimulated (rather than intimidated) by the prospect of broadening the definition of *cognition*, I found it comfortable to deem the capacities of those in the arts as fully cognitive – no less cognitive than the skills of mathematicians and scientists, as viewed by my fellow developmental psychologists.

Rogoff *et al.* (1993) describe problem solving, emphasizing its lifelong quality, as follows:

> The purpose of cognition is not to produce thoughts but to guide intelligent interpersonal and practical action. A problem-solving approach places primacy on people's attempts to negotiate the stream of life, to work around or to transform problems that emerge on the route to attaining the diverse goals of life.

Throughout the Foundation Stage early years practitioners are helping children to set up the potential for the unguessed connections which will be needed for the many structures which will be required throughout the child's lifetime. In the introduction to their book about the brain, Ramachandran and Blakeslee (1999) quote the following words from Laurence Miller:

> By the deficits, we may know the talents, by the exceptions, we may discern the rules, by studying pathology, we may construct a model of health. And – most important – from this model may evolve the insights and tools we need to affect or own lives, mold our own domains, change ourselves and our society in ways that, as yet, we can only imagine.

Taking account of the locality: children's contexts

An important part of children's contexts is inevitably the people and cultures within which they live – both of these things shape children's learning (Rogoff *et al.* 1993) and because they are learnt early they are not readily unlearnt (Siegel 1999). In early childhood education, practitioners claim to be well aware of what is often termed 'what the child brings with him or her'. All too often the pressures described earlier in this chapter mean that teachers may not act on this knowledge, but may be led to feel that ploughing on in the predetermined direction will achieve faster results. And that is often the problem. What Hughes's seminal text on mathematics, published in 1986, demonstrates all too clearly is that if children's initial levels of understanding are not directly addressed, progress is severely curtailed.

One of the challenging and exciting aspects of working with young children is that because their experience is necessarily limited by their age – how much can anyone do in thirty-six months? – their understanding is bound to be idiosyncratic. What experience in a group setting has to offer children, above all else, is the opportunity to learn from the experiences of others. In order to do this, children need two things. First they must feel that their experience is acknowledged, visible and valued. Second they must be supported in finding links between their own experience and that of their peers. This has the advantage of enabling children to build on existing understandings and to become more open-minded to change and difference. Both are vital elements in creating foundations for a future which is uncertain. Again, it is interesting to note how much a part of the tradition of early childhood education this desire for open-mindedness was. Lowndes (1960: 83–4) cites Dame Sybil Thorndike's writing about a country house established for the children of Deptford:

> There was such a happy, friendly atmosphere, and we all particularly loved the way children of other [*sic*] races and colour were treated. All were one big family, and it seems to me that by the McMillan spirit we may look forward in the future to men and women who will have learnt in their childhood that all colours and races can be real brothers and sisters.

When children first arrive in a group setting, prejudices and stereotyping may be a prime mode of coping. We all use categories to help us to deal with large amounts of new information and a child's first time in a nursery will bombard them with new people, adults and children, new social rules, new objects and routines. In seeking to establish themselves within the groups and retain their own sense of identity they may overemphasize their gender qualities or choose to link with other children who appear to have similar qualities or characteristics. While teachers and other practitioners should understand this they should not accept it as simply normal or natural. If we are to create foundations for lifelong learning and personal development, children must be helped to see beyond superficial and often physical manifestations of difference. Paley (1991: xii) describes this process in moving words:

> The story of Jason and his helicopter reminds us that every child enters the classroom in a vehicle propelled by that child alone, at a particular pace and for a particular purpose. Here is where the fair study of children begins and where teaching becomes a moral act.

Physical environments and foundations: effective environments for learning in the Foundation Stage

The foundations needed for long-term development and lifelong learning have to be flexible, long-lasting and strong enough to withstand unforeseen changes and pressures. An effective environment for creating foundations of this sort must equip young children to deal with the future.

When we consider the site and locality of learning it is clear that we should be celebrating young children's remarkable capacities. The blueprint for human development has taken thousands of years to adapt to humans' ever-changing way of life. An emphasis on movement is fundamental to learning. Song, story and dance are from our earliest days essential ingredients in the human learning process. The long childhood which has evolved in humans exists because it allows us plenty of time to play and explore, to experience and hypothesize. These activities will feed and develop the connections in the brain which form the foundations for future adaptive and flexible learning. Our long childhood further dictates that children learn best when they are encouraged to make use of their cognitive fluidity and their senses to learn – making connections between all areas of the brain and all kinds of experiences.

The staggering competence which babies possess at or very soon after birth should increase our respect for them as learners. Young children must not be hurried through the vital social aspects of learning. Above all we should ensure learning environments for young children which:

- respect and acknowledge their prior experiences – recognizing the lifelong value of a long and playful childhood;
- ensure a rich range of experiences which open their minds and bodies to new possibilities;
- promote inclusive social interaction – helping children to make meaningful connections with others – for human minds work best when linking with other human minds (Siegel 1999);
- allow children to feel safe enough to dare to take risks and make mistakes – for without this children cannot develop as independent learners;
- make children reflective and aware of their own learning (and that of others);
- give them tools for thinking – what in Reggio Emilia are termed *the hundred languages of childhood* (Edwards *et al.* 1995).

Conclusion: taking time and making space

The space created for the foundations of a building has breadth and depth. Without taking the time to create firm footings, the structure of the building will not be secure. The foundations which are laid by young children for lifelong learning also require time and space. The creation of a firm foundation cannot be rushed. Early childhood practitioners have been, and in many ways remain, under pressure to accelerate the process of learning. In this country a child can be deemed to be failing as a reader at an age when in most other countries they would not be expected to read. There is no evidence that an earlier start pays off in the long run.

The bywords of the McMillan sisters in their work with the socio-economically disadvantaged groups of children and their families with whom they worked in Deptford were *time and space*. Children living in homes described by the McMillan sisters as cramped, damp and dismal had little space in which to run or time to reflect in tranquillity. The sisters in their work set out to create time and space in order that children could thrive and grow in body, mind and spirit. When they saw that germs were the foes, they created time and space to act on these things. Similarly we have to create time and space – not for the foes identified by Margaret McMillan but to allow children (and those who have the privilege of and responsibility for working with them) to find effective ways to cope with today's challenges.

The wide range of contemporary pressures placed on young children and their families mean that children need time and space to deal with their anxieties. They need time and space to take some risks – not an easy thing to do when you feel insecure. Above all they need time and space to think. Taking time to think, Claxton (1997) reminds us, does not always involve more time – it simply demands unpressured time.

The remarkable competence shown by babies should not lead us to squander or exploit their learning. It should make us humble enough to recognize that we do not fully understand the processes that are at work. The neuroscientists have joined early childhood practitioners, writers and theorists in recognizing the vital importance of children's 'magical thinking' (Paley 1981: 4); 'ecstatic responses' (Egan 1988: 86) and 'slow ways of knowing' (Claxton 1997: 3). We must use the opportunity provided by the introduction of the Foundation Stage to create stress-free situations where the imagination can run wild and where intuitive leaps of understanding can occur. Thinking and risk taking in a safe environment will make it possible for children to act independently and flexibly in order to face a future of constant change, calmly taking the time that it needs to build the foundations that will last a lifetime.

TWO

High levels of achievement for young children

☐ MARGARET EDGINGTON

Introduction

As a society we are rightly impressed by, and proud of, high levels of achievement in all fields. The hordes of people who flock to sports events, art galleries, museums, concerts, plays, and so on, do so because they wish to experience excellence. Parents want their children to become rounded individuals who have the chance to reach their full potential in as many fields as possible. Many of the increasing number of parents who opt to educate their children at home (Thomas 1998) or send their children to private schools are now doing so because they do not wish to see their child's opportunities narrowed at an early stage in their lives.

In this chapter the notion of height in education will be defined broadly. When we think about height in education we should not just be concerned with those high-fliers who achieve excellence in their fields; we should also aim to enable all young people to become lifelong learners. Successful education enables children to want to go on developing and learning throughout their lives. Height will be defined to include high levels of development or achievement in the areas of:

- citizenship – personal and social development;
- mental health – emotional intelligence;

- basic skills – relevant to language, literacy and numeracy;
- physical health;
- creativity – relevant to the arts and to the fields of science and technology.

Achievement in all these areas is being threatened by an education system which is skimping on the foundations of experience and learning. It is likely that damage to development in one area will have a negative effect on development in the others. If we want our children to do well in a particular field, we must simultaneously ensure that they thrive as people.

Developing good citizens

Good citizens are those who feel connected to, and are motivated to make (in collaboration with others), a contribution to the community in which they live. They have a strong sense of responsibility to themselves, as well as to others, and show interest, respect and tolerance in their social relationships. They can show maturity by working for the common good, even if that is not what they originally wanted themselves.

It seems that employers, when seeking to appoint staff, look first to those individuals who can demonstrate the qualities of a good citizen. An analysis by the University of Sheffield of the kinds of qualities sought by prospective employers of graduates identified ten skills and qualities most commonly identified in newspaper job advertisements (see MacBeath 2000):

1 oral communication
2 teamwork
3 enthusiasm
4 motivation
5 initiative
6 leadership
7 commitment
8 interpersonal skills
9 organizational ability
10 foreign language competence.

All, except the last, fall within the personal and social domain – and even the last is essential in making positive relationships with international colleagues. While these skills and qualities have been squeezed out and become a luxury in the overburdened primary and secondary curriculum (Perkins 1998), they have been traditionally exceptionally well supported within early years settings. However, Sylva (2000: 133) warns that there is evidence in England and Wales that 'there has been a progressive move towards more formal learning especially of early literacy and numeracy'.

This is serious, since evidence from research shows that early education programmes which 'encourage the development of emotional, cognitive, social skills and feelings of self-efficacy through natural activities such as play and exploration result in lasting social and educational benefits, especially for children from deprived backgrounds' (POST 2000: 12). American research highlights that children who have experienced 'direct instruction' (characterized by a teacher-led approach, involving lessons with clearly defined academic goals in terms of reading, writing and arithmetic) have significantly more social problems and demonstrate more delinquent behaviour in adolescence and adulthood than children who have been offered opportunities for autonomy and self-direction (Schweinhart, Barnes and Weikart 1993). Sylva (2000: 133) recommends a shift towards a 'more social curriculum'.

The *Curriculum Guidance for the Foundation Stage* (QCA 2000: 8) emphasizes that practitioners should plan a curriculum which supports, fosters, promotes and develops children's

- personal, social and emotional well-being;
- positive attitudes and dispositions towards their learning;
- social skills;
- attention skills and persistence.

The approach to learning and teaching outlined in this Guidance has been widely welcomed because it reinstates the importance of this area of development in underpinning all other learning, and because it emphasizes play as an essential vehicle for learning. However, many practitioners working with children in the Foundation Stage are inadequately trained and lack the knowledge of child development which would enable them to identify personal and social needs and offer appropriate support to individual children. Practitioners who develop a content- or outcome-led curriculum do not usually give sufficient thought to how they will introduce this content to cater for different learning styles. Motivation and interest are important in learning at all stages and there is evidence that some children are being 'switched off' from learning because they are being asked to engage in activities which they find boring and/or difficult. Boys, who often need a more active approach, and children who are developmentally less mature (or simply younger!) find sitting still especially difficult and are particularly disadvantaged by an undifferentiated, adult-directed curriculum. These children may develop a sense of failure and may stop wanting to try. Dweck and Leggett (1988) emphasize the importance of children developing a sense of 'mastery' and a willingness to persist in the face of difficulty or challenges. If children are regularly given tasks which are meaningless, uninteresting or too difficult for them, they may become 'helpless' and alienated from society by the time they reach adolescence (or earlier).

Play is a powerful motivator of young children, but within a predominantly female profession play experiences on offer and valued by adults may reflect female interests more readily than male concerns. Gender divisions in play are increased by the influence of television and advertising (Carlsson-Paige and Levin 1990), with the consequence that boys are motivated by play that is more active and physical and often involves weapons. This type of, often boisterous, play is frequently regarded as inappropriate in a setting where passivity and quiet sitting is valued. Female practitioners try to divert the play but may not connect with the boys' interests e.g. the diversion of Ninja Turtle play towards cooking pizzas misses the point that it is the action of the play that the boys find attractive. On the other hand setting up a police station out of doors with police officers' notebooks proved very motivating in one setting and involved even the most reluctant mark makers in writing arrest warrants! Catering for different learning styles requires practitioners to embed the curriculum content in the child's preferred activities rather than removing the child from his/her preferred activity to the curriculum content. This way children feel respected and valued and are more likely to maintain involvement in the group.

Relationships are deeply significant in early learning. The successful Perry Pre-School Project in the United States (Hohmann *et al.* 1979) was characterized by high levels of parental partnership and by pre-school staff who engaged in a dialogue with children. This idea of a dialogue is also in evidence in the Reggio Emilia nurseries in Italy (Katz and Cesarone 1994) where adults support children to develop their ideas collaboratively. Oliver and Smith (2000: 29) assert that 'an adult–child relationship which is exploratory and supportive in nature leads to higher levels of self-esteem in children'. Sadly, early years practitioners

currently feel that they have little time to develop these supportive relationships with children and their parents; 'they want to
be able to focus on children as individuals and to allow them
simply to be children (rather than feeling they have to push
them towards unrealistic and irrelevant targets)' (Edgington 2000:
17). There is little doubt that young children learn a great deal
about what it means to be a citizen in wider society from their
nursery and school experiences. If their concerns are never
noticed, let alone valued, by adults, they build up an image of
themselves as unimportant and may ultimately opt out of the
group. The increase in behavioural problems in school is almost
certainly exacerbated by inadequate, unsupportive provision of
this kind.

If we truly wish to aim high when developing the citizens of
tomorrow we need to ensure that:

- personal and social development is explicitly planned;
- Foundation Stage settings encourage all children to make
  choices, take responsibility and feel a sense of community;
- adults make time to get to know individual children by observ-
  ing and listening to them and to develop responsive, collaborative relationships with them;
- the approach adopted to personal and social development in the
  Foundation Stage is continued and developed throughout the
  primary school and beyond, keeping in mind throughout
  the Early Learning Goals that children should 'continue to be
  interested, excited and motivated to learn' and 'work as part
  of a group or class, taking turns, sharing fairly, understanding
  that there needs to be agreed values and codes of behaviour
  for groups of people, including adults and children to work
  together harmoniously' (QCA 2000: 32 and 36).

Ensuring mental health and emotional intelligence

Mental health is dependent on adults having high self-esteem
which enables them to demonstrate inner resilience in the face
of difficulty or challenge. Emotional intelligence requires people
to be self-aware, able to control impulses, persistent, motivated
and able to show empathy for others (Goleman 1996). Many of
the factors and strategies quoted above, which support children's
growth as good citizens, also support the emotional area of development. As we saw, these have been neglected in recent years.

There are signs that the state of mental health and emotional intelligence in Britain is not good and there are strong indications that it is getting worse.

The Mental Health Foundation (1998) has highlighted that the rate of diagnosable mental illness among children between the ages of 4 and 18 is approximately one in five. An increasing number of men commit suicide. There have been a number of well-publicized cases where teenagers (including girls) have committed suicide, at least in part as a result of the pressure on them to succeed or do well in examinations. There is a clear connection between societies (such as Japan) which place high value on narrow academic achievement and high suicide rates among young people. Additionally, the European School Survey carried out by the University of Edinburgh in 1999 reveals that Britain has the worst record out of 30 European countries for youngsters using addictive substances such as tobacco, alcohol and drugs. It is interesting that parents are blamed in the press for their children's lack of control and for not supervising their children properly.

However, many of today's adults remember their years of childhood (throughout primary school) and adolescence as being ones where they had a tremendous amount of freedom from adults and often played outside with others from their street for hours on end. Very often their parents had no real idea where they were or what they were doing – they simply trusted their children and gave older ones responsibility for younger siblings. Although some of these trusted children can remember occasionally getting into difficulty, they also feel that the freedom they were given taught them how to assess risk and to walk away from what was obviously not a good idea. They also remember that they were rarely bored. Perhaps it is the fact that children are so over-protected today at primary age that they are unable to cope when they are finally given some freedom in their teens. Lindon (1999) points out that we cannot and should not attempt to take all the risk out of children's lives. She makes it clear that 'Adults who analyse every situation in terms of what could go wrong risk creating anxiety in some children and recklessness in others' (1999: 10). Within today's society, where the 'risks' are perceived to be much greater than for previous generations, young children have little opportunity to play away from adult supervision. Many children go from nursery or school to organized clubs or lessons leaving very little time for free play with peers or siblings.

Bruce (1996: 1) argues that 'play has a long term impact on adult life. It becomes a resource which can be used in later life to:

- deal with setbacks and tragedies;
- live a full life;
- make a major contribution to mental and physical health;
- give a sense of well-being and control;
- help make sensitive, sound relationships with people;
- be creative and imaginative.'

Although the need for children to learn through play has been highlighted within the Foundation Stage Guidance, the reality in practice is that much play provision is poorly planned and resourced and many adults do not understand how it can support children's all-round development. Many reception classes have become dominated by tables and chairs and teachers are having to rethink their organization and daily routine. There is also pressure on practitioners to validate play by identifying learning objectives for all play provision in their setting, but this risks turning 'play' into something unattractive to children. As a nation we need to understand the possible long-term effects of starving children of the chance to direct and be in control of their own play and to enjoy their play experiences. If they are not having these opportunities at home then they must be on offer in early years settings. 'We should be wary of depriving children of opportunities for enjoyment in the present' (Oliver and Smith 2000: 55).

Children use play as a vehicle for exploring ideas, feelings and relationships as well as materials. Work on feelings is particularly important if we want children to grow into mentally healthy adults. Goleman (1996) points out that many children are not effectively supported within their families and that emotional literacy sessions should become part of the school curriculum supported by sessions for parents so they can 'deal more effectively with their children's emotional life' (p. 280). He goes on to say that 'the optimal design of emotional literacy programs is to begin early, be age appropriate, run throughout the school years, and intertwine efforts at school, at home and in the community (p. 281).

Oliver and Smith (2000: 55) also stress the need to develop parents' self-confidence in supporting their own children and conclude that 'a problem-solving curriculum, in which a relationship of dialogue with the adult is fostered, appears to increase the child's sense of achievement and confidence and reduce shame . . . Supportive interest and concern, not overlaid by authoritarian strictures, appear to work well with both adults and children in that they help to strengthen inner resilience and self-esteem.' There are equal opportunities considerations here, particularly in relation to families who speak languages other than English or who come from diverse cultural and religious backgrounds. In order to support children and parents, bilingual practitioners are required, who have understanding and respect for the families' heritage and traditions (including child-rearing practices) and are capable of explaining, without patronizing, what the setting is trying to achieve. All children need to feel that they and their family are respected and valued and that the setting or school positively welcomes them. Children and parents also need to know what the setting's aims and expectations are so they are clear about the new community they are joining and their role within it (Drury 2000). These aims must include a zero tolerance of bullying and discriminatory practice if all children are to flourish in the setting.

Aiming high in basic skills of language, literacy and numeracy

Basic language, literacy and numeracy skills are essential in everyday life and any modern society depends on having a population who can communicate effectively, read, write and interact confidently with numbers. There are quite simply few opportunities for the illiterate or innumerate. It is, therefore, not surprising that the government has prioritized these areas for intensive focus through its literacy and numeracy strategies. There is evidence from SATs results that these strategies have been successful in raising standards at the end of Key Stage 2, although writing, and in particular boys' writing, is an area where less progress has been made. There is, as yet, no evidence of the long-term effect on achievement of those who were introduced to the strategies in the early years of their schooling. It is quite possible that short-term gains in the early years of schooling will translate into a depressing of results in the later years. Evidence from research shows that

> skills such as reading writing and maths require teaching, but there is no convincing evidence that teaching these skills

early (before about six) is advantageous. International studies suggest that a later school starting age (age six or seven) might be beneficial if school is preceded by high-quality pre-school education.

(POST 2000: 12)

Anecdotal evidence from teachers and headteachers suggests that high levels of achievement at the end of Key Stage 1 do not necessarily lead to high levels of attainment at the end of Key Stage 2. This seems particularly to be the case in literacy, where there is widespread agreement that some of the aims for the end of the Foundation Stage are unrealistic for children who may still be 4, and incompatible with the goals for the other areas of learning. It is alarming and sobering to hear a reception teacher on a course reporting that she has to put any child who cannot recognize at least 10 of the 45 high-frequency words identified within the Literacy Strategy Guidance (DfEE 1998) on the Special Educational Needs register. If these children were being educated in another European country they would not be expected to start reading until at least 6 years of age. Many home-educated children start to read late but still become competent readers with a voracious appetite for books (Thomas 1998). The central question here is are we more concerned that children can identify specific words or letters early, or do we ultimately want them to be enthusiastic readers? An approach which over-emphasizes letter and word recognition at the expense of developing positive atti-tudes to reading is one which will doom many children to a life where they can read but gain no pleasure from doing so.

The relatively low priority being given to the development of speaking and listening skills is also a cause for concern, particu-larly as many children in the Foundation Stage have limited or delayed language skills and often find it difficult to listen. Many children, particularly but not exclusively boys, are reaching adult-hood unable to express themselves clearly and rationally. The evidence of this is to be seen in the numbers of teenagers and adults who have no other communication strategies except swear-ing and physical aggression.

Communication skills are essential in our social lives, but they also lay the foundations for literacy. Holdaway (1979: 12) asserts that 'A traditional error of thinking about reading and writing was to see them as discrete subjects isolated from the world of language and spoken culture and then to teach them as if they had no relationship to listening and speaking.' It is quite clear to any experienced writer that writing is first and foremost a linguistic activity. It involves expressing ideas in language and then transcribing them. In other words it is not primarily to do with the physical skill of holding a pencil. In the Foundation Stage children first need support in expressing their ideas and stories in language – when appropriate an adult can act as a scribe and show the child that his/her words can be captured in print. They also need to have the chance to 'have a go' at writing for a purpose in real contexts e.g. writing shopping lists, keeping score when playing skittles. In this way they become interested in writing and want to engage with it. If they are expected to form letters correctly when they are physically incapable of doing so, they will experience a sense of failure and will not want to try. As a physical activity, writing is tiring for young children, particularly for boys. If they begin to find it too hard in the early years it will be difficult to motivate them later. The fact that boys' writing in the primary school is a cause for concern comes as no surprise to early years specialists – it is almost certainly rooted in inappropriate approaches which have been imposed on nursery and reception practitioners.

Another problem for young children occurs when they are asked to engage with literacy or numeracy activities in disembedded contexts where they cannot see the point of what they are doing. This was one effect of the introduction of literacy and numeracy hours or lessons. Katz and Chard (1989: 43) point out that 'the content of interaction and activity is likely to engage children's minds when it is related to what is salient and familiar to them.' The Numeracy Strategy Guidance (DfEE 1999) is of less concern because it emphasizes the need to plan lively interesting experiences and because it emphasizes mental and oral (as opposed to written) approaches to number. The Guidance for this strategy has also made it clear that teachers can cover the elements of the 45-minute numeracy lesson over the day in an integrated way. The Literacy Strategy Guidance makes this less clear although subsequent guidance from the DFEE and within Ofsted (2000) guidance gives responsibility to Foundation Stage teachers to plan in a way that suits the developmental needs of their group. The introduction of literacy hours and numeracy lessons in reception classes has been very damaging to many children's disposition to learn. The separation of subject areas, the over-directive style of teaching, and the length of time children were expected to spend sitting on the carpet were inappropriate for all young learners but particularly damaging for boys, the least mature and youngest children, children learning English as an additional language and children with special education needs. The fragmentation of time was also unhelpful. Young children (and indeed all learners) need uninterrupted time to work in depth (QCA 2000) and to wallow in their learning. The literacy and numeracy lessons, when rigidly introduced, dominated the daily routine so that children had no opportunity to work in depth on literacy or numeracy or on anything else. The routine in many reception classes returned to the 'work in the morning, everything else in the afternoon' pattern, which has been considered inappropriate in the past. However, on a more positive note, both strategies focus attention on the range of content and experi-ences children need to access in order to become numerate and literate. In that sense they are helpful, but only if practitioners are enabled to introduce the content and experiences in ways that are relevant, and appropriate, to the needs of their group of children.

> The available studies suggest that early reading, writing and maths experiences can be valuable, as long as they are embedded in children's preferred experiences and interests and are not too formal, abstract or disconnected from other activities. There is some evidence that pressurising young children to learn about letters or numbers in too formal a manner might be counter-productive.
>
> (POST 2000: 12)

It is now time to take stock of the impact of the strategies on young children's learning. If we wish all children to aspire high in this area and to become able communicators and keen readers and writers, there urgently needs to be a review of the Early Learning Goals for Communication, Language and Literacy and the Literacy Strategy Guidance. Higher priority should be given to communication, speaking and listening skills in the Foundation Stage, but there should also be a recognition of how children's emergent reading and writing skills develop in meaningful contexts. Children may well be able to read and write many words by the end of reception but these are most likely to be words which are personally relevant.

This review would of course have an impact on Year 1. The Guidance for Key Stage 1 also needs to be reviewed to ensure that children can build on the more solid foundations built in nursery and reception settings. We should be aiming less high at the end of Key Stage 1 in literacy and numeracy in order to achieve higher levels later on.

Promoting physical health

Aiming high in this area of development is not just concerned with the minority of people who will become record-breaking athletes, prize-winning sportsmen and women or leading dancers. It is also about ensuring that everyone maintains a healthy active lifestyle and maximizes their chance of a long and productive life. It is costly to society to put right illnesses which may never have developed if people had taken better care of their bodies. Children need to become aware of what constitutes a healthy diet and lifestyle and need to understand the importance of, and be motivated to participate in, vigorous physical activity.

Bilton (1998) points out that changes in lifestyle mean that most children and adults no longer have to engage their whole bodies in everyday activities. Before the advent of the car and labour-saving devices everyone walked or cycled more and generally engaged in more physical activity in the course of their daily routine. In today's society the television, video and computer dominate, and lifestyles have become more sedentary and more indoor-based. Children can no longer play outside freely with their friends and many live in cramped conditions without gardens (or with gardens that have been inspired by the garden makeover programmes on television and have consequently become show-pieces for adults!). As a consequence of this lack of activity an increasing number of children are now obese. Latest figures suggest that one in ten children under the age of 4 are overweight, and, of those, one in four are obese.

In their formative years from birth to 5 when a huge amount of physical development takes place and when lifestyle patterns are being established, it is particularly important that children are encouraged to be active. Outdoor provision in Foundation Stage settings is crucial in providing space and opportunities for children to operate on an active scale. In 1914 when Margaret MacMillan set up her nursery school in Deptford the concern was to set up an 'open air' learning environment with shelters to support the work in the garden. At a time when many children were living in poverty it was considered vital that the emphasis should be placed on good nutrition and being out in the air. In more recent years, with the push towards more passive styles of learning and with many practitioners ill-trained to understand the importance of outdoor learning opportunities, the use of the outdoor environment has declined. The many children in reception classes have often had no access to an outdoor space except for playtime where they have had to cope in a large space with many much older children. This is of great concern when many children are leading lives which are relatively just as disadvantaged as the lives of the children of 1914. It is arguably more important than ever that children should be offered a physically active outdoor curriculum. If we do not enable children to be active learners we risk damaging much more than their physical health. We also threaten their development in writing and in the creative area of development. Children's fine motor skills involving holding pencils, hammers, paintbrushes etc. are refined from gross motor skills. If children are denied opportunities to develop control of their whole bodies they will be disadvantaged when they need to control tools.

The *Curriculum Guidance for the Foundation Stage* (QCA 2000: 15) emphasizes that practitioners should 'make good use of outdoor space so that children are enabled to learn on a larger, more active scale than is possible indoors'. This is a challenge for many practitioners, first because some have not got easy access to an outdoor space, and second because many do not understand how to develop a stimulating outdoor environment. Another constraint is time. Young children need time out of doors if they are to develop their ideas in depth and engage their whole bodies purposefully. When time is limited to a 20-minute session when the whole group go outside, the most eager children (often boys) will tear around on foot or tricycle letting off steam, while the more nervous children (often girls) will cower round the edges or stay near to the adult. This early experience may well be at least partly responsible for the fact that many girls choose to give up sport as soon as they can. Practitioners must recognize the long-term importance of outdoor play and see the outdoor environment as an extension of the room. Children should have some time each day when they can move freely between the inside and outside areas. This enables children to integrate different types of learning and also ensures that the more timid children are able to go outside without having to contend with the whole group.

Developing creativity

High fliers in all fields (not just the arts) demonstrate a degree of creativity. Creative people are imaginative, see possibilities, are not afraid to try out new ideas, are persistent and do not give up when faced with a problem. They are risk takers who constantly seek to stretch the boundaries and find innovative ways of approaching things. Genuine creative geniuses show great perseverance over the long haul and do not necessarily depend on prodigious childhood skills (Howe 1999).

If as a nation we aspire to excellence, we must ensure that our education system actively promotes creativity. Sadly this country's recent track record is not encouraging. Although successive governments have claimed that they value and wish to encourage creativity, recent policies have not reflected this. Creative writing is suffering because of the constraints imposed by the literacy hour. The arts have been marginalized in a system which strives for standards in more easily measured areas of learning and therefore gives most time to basic skills development. Science teaching in primary schools often fails to engage children as scientists – presenting science as a knowledge base to be learnt and regurgitated in SATs tests rather than as an exciting discipline where the knowledge base is constantly being challenged and revised by creative and persistent individuals.

Teachers would argue that they can do little else in the time they have available to them. SATs tests apply only to English, maths and science with greatest value placed on the first two. It is inevitable that teachers, concerned about results, league tables and performance management, will give greatest priority to those aspects of the curriculum which are to be measured. The constraints on time seriously affect children's opportunities to engage in depth in the process of exploring ideas, materials and feelings for themselves without any requirement to produce an end product or piece of work. Very young children will wallow in dripping or spreading glue without any desire to stick something, and will repeatedly pour water into a water wheel and watch what happens without needing any discussion. These and many other early experiences help children make sense of their world and lay a vital foundation for later learning. Holt (1989: xvi) asserts that learning 'means making more sense of the world around us, and being able to do more things in it'. If children are denied in the early years these sense-making opportunities which come from their own creative interactions with the world around them, they will have weak foundations on which to connect more complex learning. Worse still, if children do not feel the power of their own creativity in early life they will lose this inner resource. In one nursery where the children had been used to a diet of colouring in sheets a new teacher set up a well-resourced mark-making area. To begin with not one child had the confidence to have a go at drawing or writing for themselves – they asked the adult to draw for them or asked for a colouring sheet! With gentle encouragement and a kind refusal to give them what they were asking for, the children gradually gained confidence and before long the mark-making area was the most popular part of the room. However, these 3- and 4-year-olds were at a very early stage of mark-making development because they had been denied the opportunity to experiment and practise.

Young children receive many visual images through television, video and computer games. They also see beautiful pictures in story books. These images are freely available and there is little opportunity for children to create their own mental pictures. The toys children play with may also be relatively closed as far as their play potential is concerned. There is a greater need than ever to feed children's imagination through storytelling (as well as reading) and to inspire their creativity and resourcefulness through the provision of open-ended play materials such as blocks and recycled and natural materials. Many adults remember learning a great deal from using whatever materials were to hand as play props. Many happy hours were spent deeply involved in building with sticks and stones, making perfume with petals and water, or mark-making with pebbles. There is a danger that today's over-protected children are being denied opportunities to think for themselves and see potential in even the most unpromising resource.

If children are to develop creativity they need role models who demonstrate the qualities outlined above. It is inevitable that, as teachers teach to the test and targets, their own creativity as teachers is diminished. The less children interact with creative, inspiring practitioners who are willing to take risks the less they will become creative, inspired risk takers themselves.

Conclusion

A number of common negative effects on early experience and learning emerge from the discussion above. If as a nation we truly wish to aim high in our children's learning, we need to address these urgently by ensuring that young children are given:

- time to explore and develop ideas, materials, relationships and feelings in depth;

- opportunities and time to initiate their own play alone and with others;
- space and opportunity to use their whole bodies;
- open-ended materials which encourage thinking, creativity and resourcefulness;
- positive older role models who can demonstrate the value of aspiring high in all areas of human development and learning.

The pressure to succeed in easily measurable areas of development, and the competition associated with this, must be reduced, particularly in the Foundation Stage and Key Stage 1. We must place the emphasis once again on the development of the whole person if we wish to lay the foundations from which a child can succeed later in life.

Work needs also to be undertaken with parents who, because they want their children to do well but are often unsure how to help them, are increasingly adding to the pressure. Rosenfeld and Wise (2000) highlight the dangers of hyper-parenting and over-scheduling children. They argue that the competitiveness in education has led parents to believe that children can only be gifted or disabled rather than average – if their child is not gifted at an early age then s/he must be disabled and need enrichment of some kind. They warn that in assessing or judging everything children do, we have lost sight of the fact that children are by definition unfinished – that they are not meant to be complete or excellent. We also need to remember that they may never become complete if we try to rush their foundations. Their message to parents, which is equally applicable to practitioners and policy makers, is that we should leave unscheduled time when we can just relax and enjoy time with children. Pleasure and enjoyment have a significant place in both children's and adults' lives and it is of positive benefit to human development and learning.

THREE

The impact of stress on early development

☐ MARION DOWLING

Introduction

The type of environment and education that we offer young children inevitably reflects the values and beliefs that are held by society (Dowling 2000: xiii). The current cult of achievement with its 'hurry along' pace of life places children under heavy and unreasonable pressures, both in their everyday lives and in the educational settings in which they find themselves. It is so important that, as early childhood educators, we equip children with the personal, social and emotional armour to enable them to deal with whatever comes their way.

A stressful past

Stresses in early school life are not new, as evidenced in previous educational regimes. At the height of the industrial revolution the provision of an inflexible and narrowly focused education was deemed appropriate to prepare children for life where their future work skills were predictable. Education towards the end of the nineteenth century existed in a stable and elitist society. For better or worse, children attending grant-aided schools knew who they were and where they were likely to be going in life.

Schools were first given grant aid to educate young children over 130 years ago. The imperfections of the provision are well known. There were tremendous stresses placed on infants who were crammed into desks and forced to learn facts by rote. The pressures of accountability were very evident in the days of 'payment by results' which was introduced in 1861. A description of the annual inspection in a school echoes the same effects of staff passing their stress onto children that are seen today. The inspection, as now, involved checking children's reading and numeracy skills:

> The master hovered round, calling children out as they were needed. The children could see him start with vexation as a good pupil stuck at a word in the reading-book he had been using all year or motionless with his sum in front of him. The master's anxiety was deep for his earnings depended on the children's work. One year, the atmosphere of anxiety so affected the lower standards that, one after another as they were brought to the Inspector, the boys howled and the girls whimpered.
>
> (Gosden 1969: 42)

Nursery-age children fared even worse, housed in cramped accommodation. In 1905, an inspector with the Board of Education described a nursery environment:

> Let us now follow the baby of three years through part of one day of school life. He is placed on a hard wooden bench (sometimes it is only a step of a gallery) with a desk in front of him and a window behind him, which is too high up to be instrumental in providing such amusement as watching passers-by. He often cannot reach the floor with his feet, and in many cases he has no back to lean against. He is told to fold his arms and to sit quiet. He is surrounded by a large number of other babies all under similar alarming and incomprehensible conditions.
>
> (Bathurst 1905: 818)

The approach to admitting children to school was rarely sensitive and for some children the transition to school was an abrupt and harsh experience which remained with them into adulthood. Adults recalling their early schooling in the late nineteenth century described pain: 'It was so easy to get a beating for one thing. Some boys couldn't get through a day without "holding out their hands" or a week without a real thrashing' (Gosden 1969: 43).

It is easy to condemn and look back in horror at this uncivilized and crude means of educating children. And yet the system was attempting on a very low budget (a grant of 6s 6d a year for infant children) to meet the clear requirements of society, to concentrate on the elementary skills of reading, writing and arithmetic with attention paid to moral training (Gosden 1969: 33). This training was considered appropriate for children's future working lives. There was a heavy emphasis on memorizing learning and on the obligation of duty. Little was generally known about child development. The predominant notion was of the child as an empty vessel needing to be topped up with knowledge. The works of Froebel, Pestalozzi, Montessori and Steiner were slow in making their impact felt. In the main, the system was rigid and unchanging and staff were clear about their role as educators. Apart from the wealthy minority whose parents could afford for them to go further in education (and after 1907, able children who passed the scholarship system to gain a free place at secondary school), the majority of children spent a largely tedious elementary school career being 'filled' (or not) with just sufficient knowledge to prepare them to become effective workers. They were expected to be passive recipients of an educational process in which they took no active part. The main pressure was to conform; if children complied with school requirements they could eventually expect to be fitted into predictable positions in work and society. When they left at 11 or 12 years they encountered a world of certainties. They could take for granted that some employment was available, they would be expected to marry, have children and to sustain a relationship. A clear social code was understood where everyone recognized their roles, responsibilities and standing in society.

An uncertain future

The education of young children today takes place in a totally different world. The old certainties of life have disappeared. The one certainty remaining is that we do not know what children currently aged 3, 4 and 5 years will face in the future. However, on the basis of how things are looking now, they will be living tomorrow in world of rapid change. Already we see the profound effects of the explosion of information and communication technology on people's lives, affecting the way they work, shop, communicate and live. For most people, having a job for life is becoming a thing of the past. Many people already make up their own work patterns with part-time and voluntary employment and short-term contracts. For those who follow a career, employment is global, and it is often necessary to be very mobile and move to work across continents to further promotion. In people's personal lives it is becoming possible not only to decide if and when one is going to have a child but also to select its gender, and indeed to choose one's own gender. And increasingly, the certainties and familiarities of established religious beliefs are being challenged by a huge variety of new spiritual leaders and movements offering alternative moral codes and people are being increasingly left to make their own decisions about how to conduct their lives. Robert Kegan in his book *In over our Heads: The Mental Demands of Modern Life* sums it up by describing the rapid move that we are making from an 'automatic' culture where decisions were made for us to a 'manual' culture where the responsibility is ours (Kegan 1994).

So, our children are growing up in a world where there is scope for plenty of choice – but also the likelihood of plenty of change. As early childhood educators, we have a tremendous responsibility to understand what it is that children will face in the future and to equip them with the necessary skills to cope with these changes. The children we are educating now need experiences that will help them to face new opportunities as a challenge rather than a threat and to be sufficiently flexible to adapt to whatever life brings their way.

There are few learning contexts in which children are more effectively challenged to think for themselves and to be flexible as thinkers and learners than in a good early years environment. Despite the downward pressures from national strategies and government initiatives, first-rate nursery practitioners continue to provide opportunities for children to think for themselves and to find their own solutions to a range of challenging problems. The foundations of learning should offer children opportunities to follow their own interests and to take their learning forward independently, through self-motivation and personal interest. It should help them organize a learning environment, which encourages independence and applauds different and idiosyncratic ways of meeting challenges and solving problems. It should provide experiences which cause children to be surprised, to think things through, to make decisions about preferred outcomes and to find solutions. Finally, it should prepare children for things to go wrong, for plans not to work, for problems to present themselves unexpectedly and for changes to need to be made. Early education should give children the confidence and flexibility to find alternative routes and solutions without this causing distress and aggravation.

The stresses of parenting

Choices can create life opportunities and changes can pose exciting challenges. However, if the pace of life gets out of control it can cause anxieties, tensions and insecurities. Parents, in common with the rest of society, face the pressures of this complex and fast-changing world. When pressures become overwhelming, family lives can prove to be stressful contexts for children. Parenting has always been a taxing job. The tremendous joy and excitement of sharing life with an emerging personality are often counterbalanced by the unremitting responsibility and exhaustion involved. Lillian Katz pointed out some particular demands on parents today.

> Many of the stresses of parenting stem from the wide range of choices, alternatives and options available to modern Americans in virtually every aspect of life. It is not difficult to imagine how many fewer arguments, heated discussions and reductions in demanding behaviour on the part of children would follow from having to live with minimal or even no choices in such things as food, television, toys, clothes and so forth!
>
> (Katz 1995: 162)

Sadly, some families do not have the luxury of having such choices. A core of families suffer because they lack life opportunities and their children are born into poverty. Financial burdens take their toll on young families; unemployment and poor housing can lead to adults having low self-esteem and seeing little point in striving for improved conditions for them and their families. A recent report published by the Joseph Rowntree Foundation showed that children are deprived of 'necessities of life' because their parents cannot afford them. For example one in 50 children does not have properly fitted shoes, a warm waterproof coat or fresh fruit and vegetables at least once a day (Rowntree Foundation 2000). The report argues though that, regardless of financial circumstance, parents try to protect their children. It suggests that spending on children is relatively similar in all families;

thus, in poorer families there is a disproportionate amount of money spent on children relative to the family income (*TES* 15 September 2000: 15). However, this struggle for economic survival can cause family members to suffer from poor mental health shown in symptoms of anxiety, depression and erratic behaviour. Such effects have dire consequences for children. Masud Hoghughi, professor of parenting and child development, suggests that approximately 15 per cent of children coming from families who are beset with these problems are, despite the efforts of schools, drifting towards social exclusion:

> Such families are unable to provide 'good enough parenting'. Their children do not receive adequate physical, emotional and social nurture, or protection from harm. They are brought up without any sensitive help to develop internal standards of behaviour; they acquire little idea of their own potential and how to fulfil it. These families do not have the motivation, resources or opportunity to help their children benefit from schooling.
>
> (Hoghughi in *TES* 12 February 1999: 2)

The role of families played little part in the nineteenth-century schools. Parents were seen to have responsibility for feeding and clothing their children. Staff saw themselves as sole educators and children's home lives and home learning were not regarded as relevant to school education. Today, nurseries and schools give a great deal of thought to ways in which they can link closely with families. There are many sensitive and successful examples of the ways in which staff and families exchange information and work in a spirit of trust for the benefit of children. Nevertheless, staff in pre-school settings and reception classes are perhaps understandably not always aware of the home lives of children and the implications that this has for learning in group settings. For example, all young children have an intense need for physical activity while their bodies are growing so rapidly. The nursery or school setting needs to be aware that their provision may be the only means of a child having access to healthy exercise where s/he leads a sedentary lifestyle at home.

A good foundation to children's early learning experiences needs to be sensitive to those children who do not receive adequate nurturing – for a whole range of reasons – and to the parents and carers who are trying so hard and yet finding things so difficult. Educators must recognize that a child who is hungry, miserable or tired will not learn effectively and has little energy to bring to the demands of a stimulating learning environment. It is important that children have the opportunity to relate to one adult as a key educator and that they, and their parents, can make meaningful relationships that will offer security and confidence in the educational setting. It is crucial that children's home and cultural backgrounds are understood and respected and that each child develops a strong sense of self-esteem and believes in his or her own abilities and capabilities. It is important to have a learning environment which offers routines and frameworks for behaviour so that children know where they are and that what is expected of them is consistent. It is necessary to understand that young learners respond best to learning situations which build on their own interests and preoccupations and that they are less likely to engage with something an adult decides is worthwhile for them. The foundations of learning can, and should, offer all of these opportunities to help children – and their parents and carers – appreciate the importance of managing their own circumstances and taking control of their own learning and their own lives.

Instabilities in family life

The stability of family life in the late nineteenth century may have been partly due to husbands and wives not being able to survive apart financially. Whatever the reason it contrasts with the turbulence of family life today. Marriage remains popular but is increasingly threatened. The total number of first marriages of both partners fell from 220,372 in 1986 to 160,680 in 1996 (Bertram and Pascal 2000: para 1.3.1). The increased divorce rate in the UK often means that children are brought up with one parent (usually the mother). There are many practical complexities of working for a single parent with young children and many necessarily become dependent on state welfare. While none of these factors in themselves necessarily harm children it can mean that, as parents sort out their complex marital circumstances, it becomes difficult for them to offer their children the undivided love and attention that is needed. Parents sometimes choose to stay together, for the good of the children, even though they are in an acrimonious relationship. This can be damaging for children's emotional lives. Daniel Goleman shows only too clearly that the way a couple handle feelings between them will have a clear effect on children, who quickly become very sensitive to the emotions of people who are close to them (Goleman 1996).

A sensitive early education should give children some very powerful strategies for dealing with the overwhelming range of emotional stresses that can come into their everyday lives. The close relationships with caring, interested adults; the opportunity to role play situations which are causing particular stress and unhappiness; the chance to discuss the situations of others through the careful selection of books and stories can all equip children to come to understand their own emotions better and to begin to learn to deal with them. These are skills that we all need to go on developing throughout life, but without a strong foundation to this learning, many adults find understanding and dealing with their own emotions to be cripplingly difficult.

The current culture of achievement

Potential stresses in family life for children are increased by the current culture of achievement. In contrast to the elitist culture of the previous century, we now live in a more egalitarian society. Until the 1970s it was accepted that the Butler Education Act met society's needs – that is, the provision of an academic education for only 20 per cent of the population (Barber 1996). There developed an increasing recognition of the waste of talent and a huge thrust in recent years to demand more in terms of achievement from all pupils. Tony Blair, the British Prime Minister, linked it to the need for economic growth. This spearheaded the move towards national targets being set for all pupils in numeracy and literacy. The present government's rationale for investing in early years education was stated in the White Paper in 1997:

> It is virtually impossible for children to make a success of their lives, unless, when they leave primary school, they can read and write fluently, handle numbers confidently, and concentrate on their work. We aim to ensure that all children have that firm foundation for their education.
>
> (DfEE 1997b: 15)

In itself that statement is not contentious. In recent years there has been substantial evidence that young children will respond to high expectations for their achievement where it is tempered with the right type of support offered by knowledgeable adults.

Nevertheless, there is a fine line between this healthy climate for learning and a climate of hothousing which only induces stress and tension. There are worrying signs of the latter. This is partly due to what schools provide for young children, but also because of pressures placed on children from anxious parents – the significant people in their lives.

All parents want the best for their children. Tizard's study of young children in the inner city showed that virtually all mothers interviewed who had children in reception classes wanted their children to have a better education than themselves (Tizard *et al.* 1988). These positive aspirations are certainly helpful for children who will feel encouraged by interest and support from their families. Despite this, in a climate of competitiveness parental interest and support can become burdensome. Several years ago, Tricia David pointed out how parents of young children had been made more anxious about their child's educational failure since the introduction of the national curriculum (David 1993). More recently headteachers have affirmed this with reports of children having home tuition in nursery schools and at the age of 5 to boost their results in national tests (O'Leary 1999). Anxieties are also fuelled by the baseline assessments on entry to school. Joan Clanchy, former head of North London Collegiate School, describes her observations of young mothers in the park with their 3-year-olds as they discuss selection procedure:

> They exchange data on the success rates of different primary schools and pre-preps, on which teachers they have decided are 'simply hopeless', on where to send Little Treasure for beginners' French, tennis, ballet, swimming, violin, and often, speech therapy . . . The time on the swing seems to be a rare moment of peace for some 3-year-olds.

Although Joan Clanchy sympathizes with the parents, who themselves are driven by the culture of 'achievement', she ends her article on a warning note:

> Most of the current small victims . . . will brush it (the pressure) all off and cope. But some will long resent the hurdles that are constantly erected in front of them and the hurt will go deep. Teenagers can exact a terrible revenge.
>
> (Clanchy 1998: 6)

Although these parents recognize the need for a broad curriculum, they are intensely competitive for their children; they are also convinced that by filling their children's lives with pre-scribed activity this will generate future success. In this respect they appear to have similar aspirations to groups of parents in some countries in the Pacific Rim. In Hong Kong, for example, parents believe that, in order to secure a future university career for their children, an early start to study is essential. Most place their children in a pre-school at 3 years, and the school is se-lected for its academic reputation. A study in 1992 showed that 95 per cent of children in kindergartens receive homework, mainly in writing and number skills. Chinese reading in 98 per cent of these pre-schools is introduced to children on entry at 3 years. Chinese writing is introduced at the same time in 95 per cent of the kindergartens, alongside English reading and writing (Winters 1998). Children are under heavy pressure to achieve in these areas with little attention being paid to personal, social and emotional areas of development. Similar regimes are found in Taiwanese kindergartens where children are bombarded by tests and lists to memorize, and face increasing pressure from competition (Murphy and Liu: 1998). But there are some worrying consequences emerg-ing from these regimes. Research reveals that, compared with similar groups in the West, pre-school children in Hong Kong show higher levels of dependency and anxiety, display more temper tantrums, suffer more eating problems and have greater difficulties with relationships. As they move into the primary sector many Chinese children do not appear to value them-selves. In Taiwan *The Republic of China Year Book* for 1997 stated that 'rates of petty crime, drug dependence and suicide (among young children) are rising' and linked these problems to 'com-petitive examinations'.

It is ironic that, while we are inclined to urge our young chil-dren to move 'upwards and onwards', the Pacific Rim countries are having doubts about their regimes which have promoted this approach. Taiwanese parents now express concern about their children's personal freedoms being denied to them as a result of a repressive educational system. Japan is a country that is rightly proud of its pupils' high academic standards. However, faced with problems of lack of creativity, competitive examinations and increasing incidences of bullying and school refusal, in 1995 Japan began to consider a new model for education. The Minis-try of Education is now grappling with the challenge of how to give children a greater zest for living and room to grow.

The curriculum guidance for the Foundation Stage has, as an early learning goal, that children should 'continue to be interested, excited and motivated to learn' (p. 32). The word 'continue' is very significant. Children come to educational settings with so much interest and excitement and motivation about learning. It is what has driven them to develop so many skills and so much knowledge in such a short life span. Early education should indeed continue this, and the foundations of learning must ensure that children have ongoing opportunities to be creative, to be inquisitive, to follow interests and passions and to sustain a zest both for living and for learning.

The pressure to keep achieving

If many parents and carers in the UK feel obliged to ensure that their young children jump through educational hoops, they feel an equal responsibility to provide for their children's leisure hours. This involves hard-earned money. The toy industry is big business as is the media which urges every little boy and girl to seek gratification from increasingly complex toys. The elaborate nature of children's toys today means that once broken they are not easily mended, which leads both to the child's distress and the parent's frustration at having wasted money. Moreover, when one considers the immense and explicit detail in many toys (play dolls in particular), it leaves doubt about the space left for imaginative and sparkly thoughts.

The biggest sales industry for young children now is in videos and CD-Roms. From a young age children commonly have a TV in their bedroom and instead of browsing through a book children can listen to the story on their computer, look at cute graphics which pop up or make noises at the touch of a button and change the storyline by clicking on an icon. Diana Appleyard, a journalist and parent of a 5-year-old, describes how parents feel compelled to purchase this software:

> Advertising blurb . . . is designed to make the parents feel paranoid. Jump Ahead Baby (a software package) suggests that you are giving your child an educational head-start, and that if you don't fork out for the new software your child will somehow come last in the race for techno-tot achievement. We are constantly told how CD-Roms will increase our child's reading age through early letter recognition and how much more 'stimulated they will be'.
>
> (Appleyard 1999)

Many would claim that these developments are simply inevitable and indeed a wonderful opportunity to introduce children at an early age to another dimension. Further opportunities for this are made possible, for example, in the first cybercafe for under-5s which was recently opened in Camden in London. Other professionals, however, express severe doubts and suggest that damaging consequences may occur if children's sensory, creative and communicative learning is restricted. Jane Healy, an educational psychologist, argues strongly that children do not need to be introduced to computers until they are 11 or 12 years old when they will pick up skills very quickly. Young children need to learn initially from experiencing the sights, sounds and smells of the real world. Healy suggests that

To replace this kind of vital experience with pointing and clicking on a two-dimensional computer screen may seriously impair brain development. The immature human brain neither needs nor profits from attempts to 'jump start' it. Simply selecting and watching a screen is a pallid substitute for real mental activity.

(Healy 1998: 27)

The richness of children's early educational experiences lies in its diversity. The first learning environment is usually the functional home, with occasional outings to the shops or the park. But, to the young child, these represent a wonderland of interest and excitement. High-quality learning environments retain this capacity to capture children's wonder and excitement. No early learning should be devoid of context or meaning. The experiences we offer children at this stage will determine how they approach learning opportunities for the remainder of their lives.

Concern for children's well-being

There are also concerns about children's physical well-being. Early evidence from a study in New Zealand shows the possible damaging effects of computer-assisted injury when children as young as 3 years start to spend long periods of time using the mouse and keyboard (reported on 'Newsweek', 26 November 2000). When young children use technology they are sedentary; time spent in front of screens means that children are not getting exercise. And yet the early years is a time of rapid physical growth and young children need to be active. The Health Board in Grampian has recognized this and launched a 'Kids in Condition' project as part of its Heart Campaign. The project offers week-long courses which include active play, playtime activities and traditional games. At present the work does not extend to pre-schools but training sessions have been extended to nursery teachers.

The 'Kids in Condition' project also considers diet. Obesity has increased in most parts of the world and figures show that the UK has an estimated two million overweight children. In the past many children may have had impoverished diets and suffered from too little food. Nevertheless, the diet was likely to be low in sugar and food would have been unprocessed. Today the junk food that is advertised and readily available seduces parents to get their children into bad eating habits. Obese children are also reported to suffer from other difficulties such as poor educational performance, social isolation and depression. After the age of 5 it becomes increasingly clear which children are likely to be obese during teenage years and in turn nutritionists can monitor which teenagers are destined to be obese adults (Blythman 2000).

Many inactive and overweight children are also over-protected. Today, parents, understandably fearful of child molesters and concerned about road safety, rarely allow their children to play outside the home or garden. One study found that young adults now aged 18 to 25 years had to wait until they were almost 9 years old before they were allowed to play outside, although their grandparents remember being free to roam the neighbourhood from about 6 years old. Furthermore, more than half of parents with children aged 6 to 11 would not consider allowing them to go to school unaccompanied by an adult before they are 10, even though a third of the parents had made the journey alone when they were 7 or even younger (*Nursery World*, 8 June 2000: 5). Social housing in cities adds to the problem. Children living in high-rise flats have little space to play indoors and no immediate access to outside play space. These findings indicate that, apart from the constraints on physical activity, young children are not having opportunities to become independent and learn about growing up with other children away from direct oversight of adults.

Young children's physical development should be of the utmost concern in the foundation years. A well-resourced learning environment will offer children opportunities, both inside and outside, to develop and practise a range of skills which will make their bodies strong and supple. Such opportunities should be the underpinning for a future in which children understand the need to be active and the benefits of remaining fit. Without the opportunities to develop physical dexterity and physical agility, many skills such as writing, understanding shape and space and using a keyboard will be harder to master.

We hear increasingly of children who are fidgety and easily distracted and who do not sleep well. In many cases this behaviour may be a signal from an inactive child who is unhappy. Until recently some practices in early years settings have compounded this problem. In particular the recent practice in some reception classes of requiring children to sit still for the most part of a literacy hour has placed many young children under almost impossible physical restraint.

Nevertheless, boisterous behaviour and sleeplessness can be difficult to cope with, at home and in group settings. There appears to be a need to label behaviour as a first step to controlling it. Hence the increasing use of the term 'attention deficit hyperactivity disorder' (ADHD) and, less common, 'narcolepsy' to describe sleep disorder. Rather than look at the underlying reasons for this troublesome behaviour, too often the response has been through the use of drugs which has caused worrying side effects including children being depressed and lethargic. The Child and Mental Health Services (CAMHS) recently reported that one in every five children suffers from mental health problems, many of which prove to be complex. In 1998–99 alone, some 500 children under 4, 900 children around 5 years and over 1500 children age 7 were seen by specialist CAMHS (Audit Commission 1999). However, the Audit Commission figures only reflect those children who received a consultation and parents who were given guidance about their child's health. Too often the response is through an easy prescription of drugs. The handout of Ritalin in England increased dramatically over five years, from about 2000 to 92,000 prescriptions in 1997 (Thompson 2000: 10–11). Department of Health figures show 157,900 prescriptions were issued in the UK last year compared to 126,000 prescriptions for Ritalin in 1998 (*Reuters Health Information*, 11 September 2000). Concerns have been voiced about hasty and ill-informed diagnosis of ADHD as well as over-prescription for the symptoms. Guidelines on the management of ADHD drawn up by the British Psychological Society suggest that current practice focuses more on trying to 'change the child' rather than consider underlying needs (BPS 2000). This response to children's signals for help surely reflects a society that is not listening, or prepared to recognize causes of distress.

The stresses of schooling

For a long time we have recognized that young children will not learn properly until they have made a secure transition to nursery or school. And yet the policy for an annual entry to school means that each year, many children who are only just 4 years old enter a reception class, which is often attached to a large primary school. A number of these children are simply not ready for the experience. Reception teachers do their best to provide for children's needs but feel under pressure themselves. For example, despite DfEE Guidance on the organization of the literacy strategy in reception classes (DfEE 2000), many teachers continue to feel obliged to introduce elements of literacy and language such as phonemic awareness and correct letter formation before children are developmentally ready to benefit.

For schools and other early years settings, the prospect of Ofsted inspections continue to be a major burden and cause of considerable stress. Despite the efforts of many well-informed and sensitive Ofsted inspectors, too many lack the expertise to evaluate the learning of and provision for young children. Where this is the case inspectors focus on only the visible outcomes of attainment and overlook the critical but more intangible aspects of young children's learning such as their autonomy, well-being and thinking skills. Ofsted has recognized the problem and is taking steps to ensure that all inspectors accredited to evaluate the Foundation Stage have a suitable background knowledge and experience of the phase. For the present, however, it is disturbing that as a consequence of inspection some early years practitioners feel compelled to act in a way which does not recognize or value the processes of children's learning.

Conclusion

Overall, young children face tremendous tensions and pressures as they strive to establish their place in the world. Certainly the stresses of modern life are not going to disappear and this calls into question how we best prepare children to face them. Children's natural resilience needs to be strengthened and this is where the affective side of the curriculum is so important. The type of person we become colours all else we do in life and the Foundation Stage of learning rightly gives primacy to personal, social and emotional development. There are grounds for great optimism as practitioners feel supported by policy makers to implement a curriculum which recognizes the need for young children to become confident, eager and independent learners.

It is important to avoid regarding young children as needy, weak creatures. Though vulnerable, they are going concerns, primed to survive and learn – but not against all odds. Having the confidence to adapt to change and to continue learning requires trust. Charles Handy suggests that

> No one will stick their neck out or take the sort of initiatives which new situations require, if they are fearful of the consequences if they are wrong. Trust, like learning, requires unconditional support, and forgiveness for mistakes, provided always that the mistakes are learnt from.
>
> (Handy 1997: 191)

The foundations of children's education must enable children to develop their trust, security, confidence and self-esteem to weather the stresses and strains that life will bring their way.

FOUR

Meeting the needs of disadvantaged children

☐ PAULINE TRUDELL

Introduction

This chapter is concerned with those children who live in poverty in Britain – an estimated one-fifth of all children (Unicef 2000) – and the sort of provision that has traditionally been made for their care and education before they enter primary school. It assesses the effect on early childhood provision and practice of recent government initiatives that have come about in the context of perceived underachievement and social exclusion, and questions whether explicit government directives for integration will be enough to achieve that unity of good practice between care and education which should form a firm foundation for children whose lives are devastated by poverty.

The influence of the past

In considering our responses to the current needs of children and their families it is necessary to trace the way in which a certain category of working-class child and family was singled out from others and provided with a different kind of care and education – education and child care that was an active shaping to particular social ends. It is the point of this chapter that this is a process with which we are still engaged. This is not to suggest a facile repetition of history, nor to ignore the profound changes that have taken place, but to acknowledge that the early development of the institutions within which we work, and those early formulations of ideas, values, opinions, beliefs and attitudes within which we are also situated, have a continuing influence. The final principle in the Foundation Stage curriculum guidance states that 'Above all, effective learning and development for young children requires high-quality care and education by practitioners.' It is salutary to reflect on how the historical organization of government departments has brought about much of the fractured reality of children's experiences today.

Over the past thirty or forty years services for young children under 5 in Britain grew in haphazard and random fashion – a mix of public, private, voluntary, day care and education services. Practitioners worked to make connections at grassroots level, many local education authorities made efforts to link provision locally, and early educationists and other powerful advocates for children and families called for a coherent national policy and system of funding (Ball 1994; National Commission on Education 1994; Pugh 1996).

Among these fragmented services and within the public sector there were two commanding forms of provision – day care and education – each with its own professional apparatus, structures of work and training, qualifications and terms of employment and each with its own tradition and divergent ideology. Each had widely differing perspectives on children and families, childhood and society. Social services day care was first provided by local health authorities and the medical and developmental perspective on child rearing joined another set of practices from social work to, together, inform that provision. Inside the other sort of state provision, nursery schools and classes, the dominant founding tradition was that of 'progressive' education – summed up in the 1960s by the first sentence of the Plowden Report, 'At the heart of the educational process lies the child' (CACE 1967).

Divisions between education and care

Although both forms of provision provided a service for working-class families, a division was apparent. Osborn and Milbank's research, published in 1987 (Osborn and Milbank 1987), found that working-class children overwhelmingly attended maintained nursery schools and classes, with local authority day nurseries used 'to an even greater degree as places of care for children from families experiencing extreme stress who had come to the attention of the Social Services Department'. That study also uncovered an enormous category of exclusion. It found that as many as 46 per cent of the most disadvantaged children in their sample had received no form of pre-school education, compared with only 10 per cent of the most advantaged. Differences in the hours offered reflected divergent positions – with most nursery education places being part-time and term-time, while day care provided (at least at the time) full-time places and extended hours. The emphasis in day care was on provision for working mothers and on care and protection, and in education on providing enriching educational experiences for children who almost by definition did not have parents who worked full-time. The principles of supplementing the good home and compensating for the inadequate one were of course entrenched in the Plowden Report (CACE 1967), which also established Educational Priority Areas.

In recent years the two major pieces of legislation affecting children and families, the Children Act (1989) and the Education Reform Act (1988), served to deepen the division between education and social services and increase inequality. The Children Act laid a duty on local authorities to protect and provide services for children 'in need'. Its implementation at a time of scarce resourcing led in a number of local authorities to a narrowing of the definition of need, for example to the exclusion from admissions criteria of the category of children of single working parents, and to the closure of some established centres.

The Education Reform Act and the introduction of the National Curriculum did not apply to children under 5 but led to an inevitable rethinking of the early years curriculum inside schools. Research published in 1992 (Sylva *et al.*) comparing the impact of the National Curriculum on day care and education provision found that in the case of nursery schools and classes the most profound impact was in the area of assessment, where there was greater continuity with assessment procedures in primary schools: that is, an ordering of observations and other information within subject areas, and a greater clarity and rigour in planning and record keeping. There was also increased liaison between nursery and primary schools, with children making regular visits to the latter prior to entry. In social services provision there was not so much staff familiarity with the National Curriculum and it had little impact of any kind (Sylva *et al.* 1999: 50):

...the children most at risk of a poor academic start to school and in greatest need of educational progression and assessment are attending nurseries where there is little curricular continuity to formal school and no staff liaison.

It is interesting that the National Curriculum brought about some improvements in the continuity of children's experiences. It is matter of national disgrace that at a time when children most need stability, security and coherence, they are most likely to get change and disjointedness. The introduction of the Foundation Stage should give practitioners many more opportunities to develop continuity across these crucial years. There are important reasons for practitioners in the various settings which any one child might encounter from birth to age 6 to liaise about ways in which they plan for, approach and assess the progress of children's development and learning. Partnership between the maintained, private, independent and voluntary sectors is being championed by the Early Years Development and Childcare Partnerships and there are greater opportunities than ever before for early childhood workers to learn about each other's experiences and expertise. The foundations of children's learning should be in environments which offer continuity of care and education from birth to age 6 – and there is a long way to go.

Children at risk

'The children most at risk ...' have a different definition in social services. To qualify now for a day care place, children in need must meet one of three categories of priority. In the first are children whose names are on the Child Protection Register, or those who without the provision of day care may need to be provided with accommodation by the authority, or children who are the subject of a court order. In the second are children with physical or intellectual disability or whose development is impaired or delayed physically, intellectually, emotionally, socially or behaviourally. In the third – and this category includes the majority of children in social services day care – are children in families who need 'professional help in caring for their child' because of their own physical or mental health or relationship problems, or 'where there is serious stress caused by social circumstances', or 'the living conditions are such that there is serious overcrowding, or the condition of the accommodation endangers the child's health or development' (Westminster Early Years Development and Childcare Partnership Plan 2001) – that is, by and large, children in poverty:

> Virtually all of the other risk factors that make rotten out-comes more likely are found disproportionately among poor children: bad health in infancy and childhood, being abused or neglected, not having a decent place to live, and lacking access to services that protect against the effects of these conditions.
>
> (Schorr quoted in Cox 2000)

There is a complexity in the way poverty is measured, and controversy and discontinuity in the way statistics are collected and presented. But, using the working definition of those whose income falls below half of the average income for the nations in which they live and whose resources – material, cultural and social – are 'so far below those commanded by the average indi-vidual or family that they are, in effect, excluded from ordinary living patterns, customs and activities' (Townsend quoted in Kumar 1993), then one-fifth of all children in Britain in the late 1990s were living in poverty:

> ... a rate more than twice as high as in France or the Nether-lands and five times higher than in Norway or Sweden. And, while child poverty has remained stable or risen only slightly in most industrial nations over the last 20 years, it tripled in Britain.
>
> (Piachaud and Sutherland 2000)

Children's life chances vary dramatically according to geo-graphical location, ethnicity, social class and parents' employ-ment expectations. Unemployment is a key factor in poverty as is low income, low benefits and single parent households. Poor families with children are more likely to live in rundown public sector housing. Health problems and developmental delay due to poor housing and nutrition, overcrowding, damp and atmos-pheric pollution are commonplace. The highest infant mortality rates correlate with high scores on unemployment and over-crowding: 'A baby from a household headed by an unskilled father is twice as likely to die in the first year as babies from households whose father is a professional' (quoted in Kumar 1993), and poor children are five times more likely to die in accidents than those from better-off families.

Helping families to work

Government initiatives to eradicate child poverty by 2020 have concentrated on helping families to work – through working families tax credit, the minimum wage and other measures – and this has indeed brought about some improvement. The independent Unicef study confirms government claims that 'the measures currently being implemented will lift 1.2 million children out of poverty by April 2002'. But, these policies will not eradicate child poverty in Britain because

> . . . about a half of Britain's poor children live in households where parents are unavailable for work – through sickness, disability or because a child is below school age – and because one in ten entering work would earn too little to lift them out of poverty. Many children will continue to depend on state benefits that currently leave them well below the poverty line.
>
> (Piachaud and Sutherland 2000)

The government's 'welfare to work' strategy has been accompanied by another, the Sure Start projects, which target special help to children from birth to age 4 in areas most at risk from poverty and social exclusion. Sure Start embraces the twin concepts of early intervention and prevention, and aims to:

- improve the social and emotional well-being of children through improving parenting skills;
- improve health, particularly through reducing the numbers of low-weight babies and a decrease in infant mortality;
- achieve speech and development that are 90 per cent normal, and improve readiness to learn;
- strengthen families and 'natural' communities.

The historical parallels are illuminating:

> It was the sight of children straying 'half naked, unwashed and covered with sores' through the filthy streets of the East End of London . . . which inspired the sisters Rachel and Margaret McMillan to devote their considerable energies to remedial work among infants . . . The two sisters rushed about on their rescue mission, dragging children out of their dark, sodden and crowded houses and trying in every way they could to remedy the deleterious effects of disease and malnutrition.
>
> (Van der Eyken 1969)

Margaret McMillan's emphasis on the physical and remedial aspects of education and her use of medical and functional theories as a frame of reference made an implicit connection between class and pathology. The construction of working-class children as existing in a state of morbidity and abnormality emerges strongly in her reference to the place of language in the education of the working-class child: 'The speech of the slums is not a dialect. It is the symptom of serious disorder, and is to be treated as a kind of deformity' (quoted in Steedman 1990). She was increasingly critical of the linguistic interactions of working-class mothers with their children: 'Many little children arrive in our schools today who are almost inarticulate. The mothers, overworked or absorbed in other matters, do not speak much to their little ones' (Steedman 1990). At the time McMillan was writing, the 'unfit mother' and the 'needy child' had long been subjects of state concern.

Urban, poor, diseased, dirty, uncared for: these were the subjects of early nursery schooling. They were also, crucially, McMillan's 'chosen sphere of political action'. Her work with children was part of a project of social change, '. . . a possible means of bringing the dangerous and debilitated, unskilled labouring poor into the fold of civilization and class politics' (Steedman 1990). This, in turn, was part of a wider project of reconstruction of the working class at a time of acute anxiety about economic decline and political instability. There was a prevailing fear that high infant mortality and the ill health and poor physique of sections of the working class would result in national decline and loss of empire. There was fear also that the extent of poverty, compounded by mass unemployment from the 1870s, would lead to public disorder. The extension of elementary schooling to working-class children was impelled by these fears. In the early part of the twentieth century public rhetoric was permeated by notions of social reform aimed at producing a vigorous and industrious imperial race and the perceived threat to the imperial vision posed by urban slums. The homes, habits, and child rearing practices of the urban poor were identified as sites for necessary intervention and reform.

It is not to disregard historical specificity to point out that Charles Booth in 1889, Sir Keith Joseph in the early 1970s, Charles Murray in the USA and at the London Centre for Policy Studies in the 1980s, and the present Labour government in the late 1990s all identify a section of the working class as being different from the rest. These are, respectively, 'the very poor, a class

of almost hopeless poverty and dependence'; the 'culturally deprived'; the 'underclass'; and the 'socially excluded'. It is a perception of the dangers of social exclusion – a perceived link with
violence and criminality and with teenage pregnancy as well as
underachievement in school – that inspires early intervention
programmes. It was such perceptions and the concern to reduce
the money spent on services for children after things had gone
wrong that fuelled the comprehensive spending review and the
establishment of Sure Start projects. Such projects have as a
central purpose the improvement of 'parenting skills' – that is,
changed patterns of relationship and behaviour within families.

Working-class children in school

The concentration of working-class children inside schools after
1870 meant that they became the location for social welfare
measures (meals and medical inspections) administered as part
of the education system. These child welfare reforms had am-
bivalent status. They could be viewed as essential to the state
disciplinary regulation of poor families, but were also part of the
programme of social reform demanded by sections of the organized labour movement – that is, the trades unions, the emerging
Labour Party and other socialist groups. They were contested from
both 'right' and 'left' political positions as state surveillance and
interference in family life.

In the late nineteenth and early twentieth centuries, when
state responsibility for the care and education of children began,
issues of infant mortality and chronic ill health among working-
class people were discussed in a context of poverty and over-
crowding, of pollution and bad diet, but the core of the problem
was widely believed to lie in faulty patterns of behaviour within
the working-class family, particularly the employment of women
and children outside the home, and in maternal ignorance and
neglect.

Part-time attendance at school was sanctioned for girls if they
helped their mothers with domestic duties. An important part of
these duties, and a vital contribution to the family economy,
was minding younger brothers and sisters while their mothers
worked. From the time attendance at school was made compulsory for children over the age of 5 older children brought their
infant charges with them. Some of those in the baby rooms of
infant schools were under 3. There was evidence to show the

harm done to the babies' health and physical development due to sitting still and cramped in confined conditions. The report by the Board of Education's women inspectors on children under 5 in public elementary schools, published in 1905, advocated 'nursery schools rather than schools of instruction for children from the worst slum homes' (Davin 1996).

The development of nursery education

Three-year-olds suffered more than physical discomfort in infant schools; the curriculum was equally restrictive. The 'progressive concentration of interest on the child' (Coveney 1967) that was a feature of the second half of the nineteenth century, together with the development of new forms of knowledge about children, had the greatest impact on the childhood of the upper and middle classes. The early subjects of scientific, medical and psychological study and investigation were middle- and upper-class children, often the investigator's own. The educational theories of Froebel and their implementation in the Froebelian kindergartens that were established in England met the needs of a growing urban middle class. Infant education in the elementary school was far removed from this enlightened practice, but Froebelian educational theory was still influential through its entrenchment in the teacher training system, although that influence was splintered and refracted through class to produce different outcomes. Isolated from their context, kindergarten techniques were introduced into infant schools as an imposed mechanical exercise. In 1892 'kindergarten' was adopted as an activity for infant children by the Board of Education and joined reading, writing, arithmetic and, 'for the little girls', needlework on the curriculum.

By the early part of the twentieth century the 'social need' for nursery schools was part of public debate. The 1918 Education Act was the first legislation to provide a financial structure for nursery schools. They were not regarded as necessary for all children. Local authorities were given discretion to apply for Board of Education grants for nursery schools for children, 'over two and under five years of age . . . whose attendance at such is necessary or desirable for their healthy physical and mental development'.

From its inception nursery education was framed by ideas of social and medical rescue. Notions of the children who were to be the subjects of nursery education were formed through their separation and division from others of their age and class. Only some children under 5 are eligible for attendance at nursery school – those who need to be saved from unsatisfactory homes and an environment hostile to their healthy development. They are the very poor, the disadvantaged, 'children in need', and the local authority's responsibility towards them is described crucially in terms of feeding and medical attention.

There is a historic connection between attempts to compensate poor children for perceived material, cultural, social, emotional or cognitive deprivation and the imposition of a narrow and prescriptive curriculum. A contemporary debate about the relative merits of 'formal' and 'informal' education for children under 5 was provoked by the first consultation document on the Early Learning Goals, during which government ministers, and others, argued that poor children required a different sort of practice. 'Nursery school goals should help children from less privileged backgrounds to acquire the basic skills they need' (John Carvel, education editor, writing in the *Guardian*, 4 October 1999).

There are difficulties with the concept of compensatory education. Behind it lurk other concepts of deprivation and individual deficit: 'Children treated as deficit systems with the shortcoming of schools put on to the shortcomings of parents and families.' Current terminology has shifted; we now speak of 'early intervention' rather than 'compensation' and 'disadvantage and exclusion' have become oddly impersonal notions. But we may not have banished all old ghosts – we still make divisions between the deserving and undeserving poor, the 'bogus' asylum seeker is a feature of our society – the plight of children who live in poverty is still too readily blamed on the lifestyle of their parents, especially if they are young and single. The specialization of childhood, the professionalization of relationships and of caring, the role of the educated expert, have all continued to develop from their origins at the beginning of the last century. Between the behavioural norms of the ideal family and what is permitted by one's own environment lies '. . . the authority of the expert' (Titmuss 1953: 9 quoted in Mayall (1990)).

Moves to integrate education and care

After the struggles of the recent past to bridge the damaging gap between care and education, and the calls for a coherent national policy and for increased funding and provision, there are now explicit directives for integration within single centres, and early childhood initiatives such as the Early Years Development and Childcare Partnerships, Early Excellence Centres, Sure Start Projects and Neighbourhood Nurseries are connected to other initiatives around family policy, parenting, social welfare, health and law and order involving the Social Exclusion Unit, Family and Parenting Unit, Education Action Zones and Health Action Zones. Each of these initiatives strives to bring much-needed continuity of experience to young children's lives and helps give them secure and robust foundations on which to build their life skills to manage and thrive. But there are dangers in that all of these initiatives exist in the context of the problem of poverty and of social exclusion, and we may be at risk of repeating old errors. New measures to combat poverty and to increase nursery provision have to be seen against the background of a long academic debate about education and inequality, of class, deprivation and disadvantage.

Increased nursery places in a variety of forms of provision and increased funding for under-5s is underwritten by the premise that early intervention will prevent later failure in school and promote social adjustment, law-abiding behaviour and community involvement. This premise rests on a body of established research, most famously the Perry Pre-School Project, that has demonstrated consistent and lasting social and economic benefits to the state from early education (Berreuta-Clement *et al.* 1984; Schweinhart *et al.* 1993). Schweinhart's cost–benefit analyses in the USA have been echoed by the national evaluation of Early Excellence Centres (Bertram and Pascal 2000) which also found that children in such centres perform better at later Baseline Assessment and better at Key Stage 1. But, although the involvement of parents is a consistent factor, the research also shows that not all forms of early childhood curriculum are equally effective. Children who experience formal didactic programmes enter school at a disadvantage. 'They can hinder young children's learning by generating higher anxiety and lower self esteem' (Siraj-Blatchford 1999).

> If we were to make evidence based policy for preventing educational and behaviour problems in children from disadvantaged communities we would recommend universal early childhood education. And on the basis of the evidence curriculum and pedagogy would shift away from the present stress in the UK on formal academic preparation and towards

the development of social skills and commitment to the learning community.

(Sylva 2000)

The *Curriculum Guidance for the Foundation Stage* rightly places children's personal, social and emotional development as the first of its early learning goals. The foundation of children's experiences must be grounded in concern for their social and emotional well-being if other more academic abilities are to flourish. The emphasis on early childhood experiences is that they should start from children's personal need and interests and, in this way, much of what is offered in our nurseries and combined early childhood centres should meet the needs of children as individuals – however demanding those needs might be. The challenge is to provide the funding and the support at the time when it is most needed – and most effective – in preventing a child from getting caught up in a damaging downward spiral of underachievement.

Bernstein (1970) famously pointed out that education cannot compensate for society. He went on to say that we 'should stop thinking in terms of "compensatory education" but consider instead, most seriously and systematically, the conditions and contexts of the educational environment'. What sort of early childhood educational context would best improve the quality of life and learning for young children in poverty and give them foundations on which they can build a satisfying and satisfactory life? The preliminary findings of the Effective Provision of Pre-School Education (EPPE) Project (Sylva *et al.* 1999) show that state nursery schools and combined centres rate consistently higher than other types of setting across all aspects of provision. 'Nursery schools with a long history of combined education and care scored at substantially higher levels than those social services combined centres with a newer emphasis on education' (Rees Jones *et al.* 2000).

This is unsurprising. Early childhood curriculum and pedagogy have been most fully developed within nursery schools. Innovative practice developed there in 'fruitful collaboration between teacher and researcher' partly 'because of the opportunities that have traditionally existed within the education system for study and reflection on work, for professional development and in-service training – a structure of education, training, inspection and advice' (Trudell 1994). A structure, alas, now broken up. But the poorest children remain in social services day care and, in the polarization of practice that mimicked the division between day care and education, the continued professional education of each group of practitioners markedly diverged.

Broadly generalized, day care practitioners spent more time considering issues of child protection and health and safety as well as certain aspects of children's familial and cultural identity. It is easy to see how clashes of professional practice arise however well intentioned the individual practitioners. For example, there is a tension between education practitioners' desire to offer children unbroken periods of time and the opportunity for uninterrupted concentration, and day care practitioners' desire to ensure that children have nourishing snacks during the day, consumed collectively as a family might. The focus on caring for children may lead to forms of practice that perpetuate dependence, while free access to outside space and encouragement to explore actively and make purposeful choices might be at odds with some children's perceived fragility. We have to redefine principles together, in an attempt to decide not what children need but what they have a right to experience (Woodhead 1997).

There is a huge onus of responsibility on those involved in training to close this divide. All adults involved with the care and education of young children need a shared knowledge base, shared standards and shared approaches. These can be supplemented by differing specialisms but there should no longer be such differences over issues that are so fundamental. The establishing of the new early childhood studies degrees will do much to prepare this foundation of learning for practitioners wanting to work in the field of early childhood but who, after their initial shared degree course, can choose to specialize among other things in care, education, library work or law.

If we were to examine the educational environment that all young children have the right to experience, we would have to consider qualities of space; time; relationships and feelings; social, cultural, and linguistic identity; and creativity. Culturally important knowledge and understanding would go hand-in-hand with the conditions that encourage confidence, optimism and a sense of mastery. Crucial to this is the informed, sensitive and reflective practitioner who plans and peoples this environment and who also ensures continuity of experience from home to nursery.

Pedagogy in early childhood education has been largely disregarded while we mulled over curriculum, but it is the quality of interaction between adult and child that defines the quality of the whole educational experience. To work in ways that fully involve and engage children and '[enable them] to construct their own understandings' (Siraj-Blatchford 1999) requires not only an initial education that covers the many different kinds of knowledge and understanding in the field of early childhood studies but also continued professional development, including time to reflect on practice. This reflection allows the role the early childhood practitioner plays in children's learning to become clearer and more explicit and ensures that the foundations are laid which enable children to achieve, whatever the odds.

The centrality of play

Such foundations would be ones that recognize, alongside other systems of representation, the centrality of play in intellectual growth, the transforming power of creative, imaginative play: 'In play, under a table or up a tree, alone or in small groups, expressing themselves in words, or with blocks, or music or miniature world materials, children think and feel and act in ways of the utmost importance for their learning' (Drummond 1996). In a later essay Mary Jane Drummond writes of children's imaginative play allowing them to 'pass through invisible doorways into alternative worlds . . . the social world of shared play . . . the realm of their own creativity' and the wider world of 'their whole society's enduring stories' (Drummond 2000). The metaphor of alternative worlds vividly cuts through the impenetrable thickets of learning theory. Bruner (1990) writes of the narrative mode of thought which is bound up with our psychic hold on reality and creates 'possible worlds' to penetrate, one of which is the world of abstract thought and language. Margaret Meek (1985) looks at children crossing and recrossing the boundaries between the real and the unreal.

It is highly encouraging that the *Curriculum Guidance for the Foundation Stage* speaks of play as a 'key way in which children learn with enjoyment and challenge' (QCA 2000: 7). But access to these worlds is not straightforward, in spite of the fact that all forms of early childhood provision in Britain appear play-based. The way in which space, time and other resources are planned in order to provide a context for imaginative or 'pretend' play will reflect the educators' understanding of its importance. Even so, it is harder for some children than others to enter the 'social world of shared play': 'Friendship and fantasy form the natural path that leads children into a new world of other voices, other

views, and other ways of expressing ideas and feelings they recognize as similar to their own' (Paley 1991). But Vivian Paley's
canon also reveals that the path may be barred to some children
and it is the task of the teacher to help them find the way in.
Full participation is hardest of all, perhaps, when the play is
scripted in a language that is not the child's own. Young bilingual learners are over-represented among the children in our
society who live in poverty and consequently in social services
day care provision (Kumar 1993), and 'Studies into linguistic and
cultural differences have not exerted much influence on the work
of early childhood practitioners' (Gregory 1997). If practitioners
are to make a difference through the use of children's play, they
must know how to plan for it, how to support and develop it
and how to observe it 'in order to have first hand evidence of
children's learning' (Fisher 1996: 106).

The following extract from the unpublished research of an
experienced practitioner who has been much influenced by studies
into 'linguistic and cultural difference' reveals the way in which
relatively small changes in practice impact on children's play
and consequently on their whole lives:

> Whilst doing some research into exactly how children's
> shared pretence play supported the development of meta
> cognition and a theory of mind, I became interested to look
> more closely at whether this premise held true for young
> bilingual children who did not share a common language in
> which to conduct complex negotiations that sustain imagina-
> tive play. I was aware too that children do not play in a
> vacuum and the context in which children's play takes place
> shapes and defines how groups of children are able to learn
> through play.
>
> The nursery contained children from a diversity of cul-
> tures and home circumstances. Fifteen out of the twenty
> two children on roll spoke a language other than English at
> home and although eight of the children spoke Arabic they
> did not use their first language in the nursery. Many of the
> parents had had to flee their home countries and were living
> in difficult circumstances: all of the children had been iden-
> tified by social services as 'children in need'. Multiple realities
> pervaded the experiences of these young children ... [I
> wanted] ... to consider how the cultural, social and emo-
> tional experiences that children bring with them into the
> nursery influence their construction of shared understandings

through play . . . This shared understanding . . . develops into a form of metacommunication which occurs when children step out of the play frame in order to communicate that what they are doing is play rather than reality. This is considered to be a high level skill in cognitive development and could therefore be seen as justification for encouraging this kind of pretence play.

In the Summer Term of 2000 the nursery was in the first stages of becoming an integrated centre. What had formerly been a social services day nursery became the responsibility of the local education department and a new team of staff consisting of teachers and early years educators was put in place. When I first began to work there, provision for the children's own free flow imaginative play was not extensive and, in the words of one of the early years educators who had worked in the nursery for some years under a different management, 'it was all down to tick lists – you had to do this and that to make sure you were covering all the activities, now we've gone back to learning through play and finding ways to help children develop how they want to – they are learning by watching each other'. Over that term the nursery class moved rooms several times, and with each move, and staff's deepening understanding of how to support the children's play, more and more space, resources and, crucially, time was made available to the children. In May I made a video of one episode of children playing with cars and the hollow blocks, which although sustained over quite a long period of time, contained very little verbal interaction or negotiation and was often interrupted by tussles over toys and space. When I went back in September to continue my research and to do more extensive videoing I was interested to discover that groups of children who did not share a common language were able to use shared understandings of experiences outside the nursery to develop their play.

(De Keller 2001)

Conclusion

Children who live in poverty require the highest quality and most advantageous early childhood educational foundations we are capable of providing, and we have a good understanding, based on research, academic study, and best practice over time, of what this should be. The continued separation of the poorest children from other children, and their placement in a form of provision that was, in turn, cut off from contributing to this growing understanding, has been a grave mistake. We have to bring to an end a system that gives poor children impoverished experience.

Integrated centres that model themselves on the best nursery school practice offer a way forward, 'Because [that practice] promotes an alliance with parents and breaks down divisions between teaching and learning and because it stresses that all learning is social and collaborative and that knowledge and experience can be shared' (Trudell 1994). Interestingly enough, recent research (Penn and Lloyd 2001) also endorses our everyday knowledge that 'many nursery schools act as a focal point for ethnic minority and/or low income communities and/or take many referrals from health and other agencies'.

But this kind of professional practice cannot be achieved through a simple amalgamation of education and day care practices within a so-called integrated centre – neither can good practice be airily 'disseminated'. All early years staff have suffered from the polarization of training and status, and there are further divisions between nursery and primary school-based staff. We require a new framework of principles and a unified practice for the Foundation Stage. Key to this process is the knowledge, experience, skills and understanding of the early childhood practitioner. The quality of education, training and experience expected of all such educators and the opportunities they are given to attain it is what will finally make the difference. With adequate investment in time, money and expertise in children's earliest years, truly comprehensive early childhood education could be achieved and the foundations of learning for all children can be robust.

FIVE

Making meaningful connections in early learning

☐ WENDY SCOTT

Introduction

This chapter is concerned with extending learning in the early years and helping children make connections between what they know and what they might learn. The discussion starts by acknowledging children's inborn drive to relate to others and to find out about themselves and their environment, and identifies some of the barriers to effective early learning. It draws on educational research and empirical knowledge about care and education in the early years, and refers to relevant recent findings about the workings of the brain. It underlines the importance of recognizing and building on young children's developing abilities in the unique context of their own family and culture, arguing that in the Foundation Stage, new knowledge is best introduced in ways which link it securely to children's existing interests and understanding. Motivation is likely to be sustained when educators relate to children's preferred learning styles and capability, and show that they too are learners. The consequent reinforcement of the disposition to learn is perhaps the most significant long-term goal of the Foundation Stage.

We are all born learners

It is characteristic of human beings to explore their environment and to reflect on what they discover. All of us construct meaning from our experience in the light of our developing understanding. The process starts at or before birth, and is never more powerful than in young babies, who are engaged from the start in trying to make sense out of the multitude of impressions they receive through their capacity to hear, move, touch, taste, smell and see. Alison Gopnik and her colleagues (1999) describe babies as scientists, testing out their ideas against implicit theories they develop and adjust in the light of their experience. The research reported provides an analysis of the relevance of adults' reactions to babies. It considers in detail the way that language development is motivated, supported and reinforced by the use of 'motherese', the intuitive way that parents and others respond to babies and extend their vocalizations with evident success. By behaving as if children are making meaning, adults support children's intention to communicate and give shape to the dialogue. Bruner (1983b) calls this process scaffolding, and describes the subtle way in which parents adjust the level of support they provide as children's capacity for independent communication develops.

This way of considering early learning as a reciprocal process highlights the importance of domestic interactions with children, and underlines the key influence of the home environment. Parents, other close adults, siblings and friends are important role models, and foster a positive attitude to learning through the way in which they encourage enquiry, and help young children to use any mistakes as opportunities for better understanding. This fosters confidence even in strange new situations, and sustains the natural curiosity which characterizes babies and toddlers.

Barriers to early learning

Negative experience at home can obstruct the healthy development of children's innate powers to learn. There is evidence that maternal depression in the early months may have a measurable effect on children's energy and confidence (Shore 1997). Stresses caused and compounded by poverty or family upheaval may inhibit parents' capacity to give time and attention to children, sometimes with disastrous results. Problems within the family do not prevent learning because children are learning all the time, but in adverse circumstances they are likely to acquire a negative perception of themselves. This has a pernicious influence on later achievement, because of the way it undermines children's confidence in relating to others, and prevents them from joining constructively in play and other group activities with their peers. The home is thus a crucial context for learning from the start, and continues to influence children's progress profoundly when they go to day care, nursery or school.

There is now a long overdue recognition that we must break the cycle of poverty and disadvantage which leads to a sense of hopelessness and despair. This welcome development has the potential to effect long-term improvements in children's life chances as well as addressing their immediate needs. Enabling families to lift themselves out of the poverty trap is a start, and initiatives to help parents gain access to health and education services are important. The drive for high-quality educational provision for all young children is especially significant for those who do not get a well-supported start at home, and is much enhanced where parents too are part of the learning. There is a need at all levels of society for a better understanding of the value of what parents and close carers, including nursery practitioners, can offer young children. In the UK there has been a limited, and limiting, perception of those who live and work with babies and infants. More widespread respect for young children's astonishing abilities would do much to establish a necessary change in our culture, and would help to assure secure foundations for children's learning, and the conditions for its successful extension.

It is essential not only to raise the profile of the early years, but also to defend children's entitlement to experiences appropriate to their stage of development. This involves reducing current inequalities within society, and also demands a better appreciation of the complexity of children's thinking in the early years. There is a need for more emphasis on what young children can actually achieve. Referring to them as 'pre-schoolers' and thinking of many of their activities as 'pre-reading' or preparation for 'real' school reveals a lack of awareness of their existing capabilities.

Although we have a highly regarded tradition of excellent nursery education in the UK, pedagogy in the early years has been a casualty of the overwhelmingly subject-centred approach to the curriculum over the past decade. Since the introduction of the National Curriculum for older children, effective ways of helping younger children to learn have been ignored in the educational debate. The Early Years Curriculum Group were sufficiently concerned about the pervasive top-down pressures exerted on early years teachers to examine the programmes of study of the National Curriculum which apply to Key Stage 1 (EYCG 1998). They pointed out that very few were in fact inimical to good early years practice. Indeed, some required children to take an active part in their learning, to interact with others, to be able to reflect and to take responsibility in ways which would enable them to link required new content to what they already knew and could do. The Group also added their voice to the many parents and professionals who were concerned about the introduction of the literacy hour, which was applied to children of 4 or 5 in very unsuitable ways. In the target-driven climate which prevailed, teachers perforce tended to use an instructional approach which did not take account of young children's learning needs.

The orthodoxy promoted by influential agencies such as Ofsted has exerted considerable pressure on practitioners over recent years. The emphasis on literacy and numeracy within a narrowed primary curriculum has resulted in an over-formal approach to the education in the early years. The loss of opportunities for active and creative involvement in learning, and of time to explore concepts and to reflect, has concerned early years specialists for some time. The introduction of baseline assessment as a value added measure and the limited range of the standard assessments at the end of Key Stage 1 are further factors which have tended to detach young children's schooling from their life experience. The view underlying this approach proposes that play, as opposed to work, is a waste of time. It reveals a serious lack of understanding of the relationship between learning and teaching.

Positive and playful approaches to learning

Effective early years educators know that it is through play that children come to terms with new knowledge and can explore and confront their feelings. Play allows them to test their ideas, and to consolidate their learning. It leads to creative experiment, and offers plenty of scope for the development of the imagination.

Kieran Egan (1991) argues that this is a profound source of mental growth in the early years. When children are in control, as they are in play, they can create their own links for new learning, and explore novel ideas and experiences in ways which make sense to them. Vygotsky (1978) asserts that, in play, it is as if a child is a head taller than himself. Certainly, free-flowing play encourages an active search for information which can be linked to existing knowledge, and recombined in creative ways. Ideas can be reframed, and unstated ideas may be inferred and developed.

An example of this, overheard on a train journey, is the way a 3-year-old played with a counting rhyme. 'One, two, three, buckle my . . . tree' she sang, several times. This was more than imitation or repetition: she had remembered the sequence of numerals, and was evidently familiar with a well-known nursery rhyme. She paused, and was nonplussed for a moment when she realized that the anticipated 'shoe' did not rhyme with the 'three' she had reached at the end of her first line. She found an elegant and satisfying answer.

Children in earlier stages of language development improvise in different ways. Esther Thomas (2000) gives some wonderful examples of words employed by her two young daughters to describe their experiences. Some, such as 'slurmey' for worms, were expressive inventions, but others were errors which made sense from the child's perspective. 'Drama trousers' for pyjamas, and 'raspberry jungle' for crumble reveal a logical use of existing knowledge applied to a new context. Thomas concludes that there are patterns in these mistakes. She points out that children tend to explore sounds in a playful way, attempt to apply rules consistently, and impose sense from their point of view by replacing a strange word with a familiar or more logical one. The delightful transformations she reports give clear evidence of her children's thinking at a stage before they had assimilated orthodox speech forms. They reveal a tendency to absorb an underlying understanding rather than specific facts or pieces of information and an ability to think creatively, beyond existing patterns.

It is notable that the two girls had their own personal ways of expressing their different associations, which were meaningful to them, and understood by their mother because she was close to their daily lives and aware of their interests and moods. This is an important factor to be taken into account at the stage when children start nursery or school. The Foundation Stage includes children up to the end of the reception year, so reception class teachers as well as nursery staff must be alert to children's previous experience and refer to their existing knowledge and cultural context as the basis for curriculum planning.

Understanding and connecting to previous experience

Katz and Chard (1989) make a clear and well-argued case for understanding and connecting to children's previous experience in their exposition of the project approach. Their propositions validate the need for educators working in the early years to find out as much as they can about each child's aptitudes, and to ensure that they stay in close touch with families, who know children intimately over time. They justify points made by the Qualifications and Curriculum Authority in the *Curriculum Guidance for the Foundation Stage* (QCA 2000), which states that a high-quality curriculum builds on what children already know and extends their interests, using varied approaches and teaching methods. This means in practice that adults working with young children will need to dedicate more time to observation, and to thinking through the implications of what they see. Many educators discover that commonly held assumptions about children's abilities underestimate what they can actually attain. Even very young children are capable of remarkable achievements when they see the point of an activity that is embedded in a context that makes human sense to them. Chris Athey's work, for example, illustrates how 3-year-olds can concentrate for long periods of time when they are following up their own preoccupations. Even where they may be apparently flitting from one activity to another, Athey (1990) has shown that they are often actively exploring underlying concepts or cognitive structures, or schemas. Her work builds on Piagetian theories of the way that new insights are assimilated into existing mental patterns, or how they may stimulate changes in understanding if a level of cognitive dissonance is reached which confronts existing assumptions. Adult learners as well as children select out from their experience what seems relevant to them, based on their existing knowledge and experience.

Vivian Gussin Paley (1988) has shown how children can be helped to come to terms with many challenges in their emotional lives, and how this can lead to intellectual growth, when supported by an expert teacher who continues to learn herself.

Paley has highly refined skills of observation and reflection, which inform her work with her kindergarten class. Her narratives demonstrate the redeeming and renewing power of imagination and play, and are a metaphor for the approach she takes as a teacher, always building on what the children show her they truly feel and think. This is not a soft option, but a rigorous discipline, far more demanding of herself and of the children than a defined syllabus, delivered through instructions.

It is important to emphasize the role of the adult in encouraging and fostering development across all areas of learning in the early years. Ensuring that new information and understanding is securely retained involves more than acknowledging children's existing experience and interests. Vygotsky (1978) has made a powerful case for promoting learning at what he called 'the zone of proximal development'. As he noted, children can do alone tomorrow what they can do with assistance today. Teaching should therefore be focused on this point of development. Bruner (1983b: 140) has characterized growing up in Vygotsky's world as full of achieving consciousness and voluntary control, of learning to speak and then finding out what it means, of clumsily taking over the forma and tools of the culture and then learning how to use them appropriately. He speaks of 'the child's capacity to use hints, of taking advantage of others helping him to organise his thought processes until he can do so on his own. By using the help of others, he gains consciousness and perspective under his own control, and reaches higher ground'.

Connecting teaching to learning

A deep interest in children, informed by good knowledge of child development, is thus an essential tool for effective educators in the early years. These attributes must be allied to an insight into individual circumstances and the capacity to recognize particular aptitudes or difficulties, so that suitable 'scaffolding' can be provided in support of children's progress towards independence. Working as part of a team, in partnership with parents, enables practitioners to compare their views with others, consider the implications of their observations, and develop their practice accordingly.

The definition of teaching given in the Qualifications and Curriculum Authority (QCA 2000) *Curriculum Guidance for the Foundation Stage* includes establishing good mutual relationships with children and their parents and carers. This acknowledges the need to provide a secure environment, and implies that adults working with young children must set aside time to find out about their existing knowledge and their personal preferences. This will help staff to 'support and extend children's play, learning and development and to plan the next steps in their learning' as the Guidance suggests.

The QCA explicitly includes planning the learning environment as well as the curriculum as part of the teaching role. Open-ended materials and resources provide versatile opportunities to establish effective links between what children already know and any new skills or knowledge to be introduced. Three children painting together, for example, may have very different aims and purposes, and will therefore respond to very different suggestions for developing their work. One may be struggling to control the brush, and be ready for suggestions about how to dip it into the pot of paint, learning next how to wipe it on the edge of the paint pot to avoid drips, and the desirability of using a clean brush for a new colour. Another may be engaged in some close observational work, representing in paint some flowers in a vase nearby. A discussion about mixing colour, and examples of other artists' work, could inspire a way forward. The third child might be exploring the capacity of red paint to cover the other colours in her painting. Adults are commonly tempted to try to save any recognizable representations before they are obliterated, but it would be wise to pause and consider whether the child is exploring the concept of covering or enveloping. This may be expressed in a variety of different ways: she may show that she is generalizing her thinking through wrapping boxes in the modelling area, tucking up dolls in beds, writing quick notes and putting them into envelopes, and then posting them, or taking an interest in dressing up in swathes of scarves. This chain of connected activity informs her concepts of space, area and shape, and could be further extended through the introduction of challenging jigsaw puzzles, tessellation, mapping, or other activities which could build on the child's exploration of covering and surrounding. Play using props such as fabrics, paper, building blocks and other materials which can be used in a variety of different ways provides an effective stimulus revealing much about the particular preoccupations of individual children. Versatile, open-ended resources nourish cognitive schemas which children can elaborate through their chosen first-hand experience.

Feeling, thinking and connecting: some indications from research on the brain

Such explorations are deeply satisfying, and this emotional dimension must be taken into account. It is all too often ignored in the educational debate. As adults, we know from our own experience how important it is to engage with learning, and how difficult it is to sustain attention when we are bored or tired. Goleman (1996) has highlighted the importance of emotional intelligence, and has put forward convincing arguments as to the relevance of feelings throughout life. It is particularly important in the early years, when children's learning is embedded in their social context, and when they are finding out how to moderate their reactions through language and logic.

Work undertaken by Trevarthen (1994) on very young children's ways of interacting with their primary carers shows how proactive even very young children are in selecting and tracking particular objects or sounds. These findings have been reinforced by recent insights reported by Shore (1997) which have begun to influence our understanding of effective ways of encouraging development. However, the realization of the importance of the earliest months and years has led to some misguided attempts to accelerate young children's achievements. The evidence suggests that although an impoverished or punitive environment hampers growth, children flourish in a wide range of ordinary circumstances, and are well equipped to make the most of the stimulus that is available through domestic routines and everyday living, provided adults who know them well take time to interact with them. In their active search to interpret new experience, human brains are very responsive to novel events. While they are processing these experiences, babies' brains are also engaged in creating neural structures which allow individuals to organize and impute meaning to what happens to them. Recent studies of the architecture of the brain reveal fascinating and complex interactions. Indeed, Susan Greenfield (1997) proposes that the human mind results from the highly personal experience of individuals, interpreted in the light of their unique predispositions and coloured by their own particular emotional reactions.

Kim Plunkett's work on the development of neural connections has led him to pose some interesting hypotheses about early learning (1998). He points out that the relationship between mental models and real life is a dialectic, and should be a continuing debate. Although science is not yet in a position to indicate clear-cut evidence about what goes on in the brain to allow particular learning to take place, we do know that neural connections change in some way in response to our experience, and these modifications of the synapses represent the knowledge we have. The brain is shaped by experience as well as shaping it. It is logical to suggest that the most effective way to introduce new learning would be to start with established neural connections, and make a bridge from known pathways into unknown territory. As Bruner says (1983b: 183), 'learning is figuring out how to use what you already know in order to go beyond what you currently think'.

An analogy in practice might be the situation of children entering nursery or school with fluency in their home language but little or no knowledge of English. From the point of view of the staff, and often their parents too, one of the main aims for such children is to improve their ability to understand and to express themselves in English. There is now a great deal of evidence that this is best achieved through maintaining the development of their home language alongside the systematic introduction of English. The complex relationship between the use of language and cognitive growth means that children can function more effectively through using their existing linguistic capacity, and that this in turn facilitates subsequent language acquisition (Gregory 1997). There are also cultural dimensions associated with the use of language which are an integral part of a child's perceptions of the world and his or her place in it. Social expectations are particularly influential in conditioning further learning, and older people are significant role models. A more explicit awareness of this, and of children's powers of imitation, could help adults consciously to adopt a wider range of teaching strategies as they seek to add fluency in English to children's existing communication skills.

Connecting practice to principle and theory

Commitment to equal opportunities is a key indicator of good practice in care and education, and demands a reflective approach on the part of the staff. It means that educators must take account of children's past experience, respecting and seeking insight into the impact of differing expectations which characterize the diverse cultures in our society, as well as the very evident individual differences between children, even those from the same family.

Imposing a way of working which does not take account of observed variation can be counter-productive: a common example is the effect of too formal an approach to literacy on young children, especially boys. Findings from research reported by Professor John Stein in connection with his work on dyslexia (lecture at the Royal Institution, 16 November 2000) indicate that boys' brains are generally slower to develop. It is therefore not logical to expect similar levels of achievement from boys and girls in relation to their ability to hold and manipulate a pencil. For different reasons, it is more difficult for left handed children to form letter shapes correctly. This does not mean that they are unable to reach expected standards, but that they will require more time in order to do so. Forcing the pace makes it less rather than more likely that they will succeed, especially if imposed practice is associated with a sense of failure or boredom, in a context which does not make sense to the child. Professor Stein quotes evidence that boys' brains are generally more plastic, and therefore more able to adapt and find alternative strategies for longer than girls can in the case of physiological damage. Loss of motivation, interest and self-esteem is however not easily replaced. As Guy Claxton notes (1997), too early, too earnest and too formal an attempt to introduce literacy may result in short-term gains at long-term cost.

For years, play has been recognized as a crucial vehicle for learning, offering matchless opportunities for testing out ideas, combining and recombining them, consolidating and extending understanding. Our own experience as adults confirms that enjoyment is more effective than punishment and pain in promoting learning. As yet, brain research tells us little about the mechanisms and impact of the chemical influences on mood and personality, but it is an area for development where evidence is being sought which can inform the debate. Bruno Della Chiesa, Director of Programmes in the OECD, is of the view that nobody will be able to decide a policy on education in the future without consulting the findings of brain research (seminar at the Royal Institution, 16 November 2000). Although others are more cautious, warning of the dangers of over-generalization (Bruer 1999), it would nevertheless be wise to draw on insights from neuroscience to help us to gain a better understanding of the complexities of learning.

It is encouraging to note that members of the Parliamentary Select Committee for Education and Employment have been convinced by the evidence presented to them during their inquiry into early learning, and are calling for the Foundation Stage to be free of formal teaching (House of Commons 2000). The report the Select Committee commissioned from the Parliamentary Office of Science and Technology (POST 2000) endorses this view, and affirms current descriptions of the nature of effective teaching in the early years (for example, Sylva 1994; David 1999; Siraj-Blatchford 2000). These theoretical arguments build on empirical thinking developed over many years, and are now increasingly informed by research, such as the longitudinal study on the effective provision of pre-school education commissioned by the DfEE (Sylva *et al.* 2000).

The government has established this major research project in support of its aim to achieve comparable quality in the provision of care and education for all young children. Recent developments in relation to special needs are particularly welcome, as they are designed to encourage early identification of any difficulties, and to establish access to specialist support where it is needed. This means that parents and practitioners will be given help in finding effective ways of introducing new knowledge to children who have difficulties due to disability, social circumstances, or other potential blocks to their learning. The consequent deepening of understanding, exemplified in a moving study undertaken over a generation ago (Axline 1964), will help the educators involved to become more effective in their response to all children.

A clear and agreed set of principles provides a reference point for the multitude of decisions parents and practitioners encounter in their day-to-day interactions with young children. They can help to resolve the conflicting priorities which are an inevitable part of life and work with a group of powerful but vulnerable young learners. Evaluating practice with reference to principles challenges the thinking of staff, and ensures that they too continue to learn. Principles form the secure framework which enables new concepts to be incorporated successfully into existing understanding, and can thus broaden the professional awareness of educators. In this sense, teachers must remain learners, and as such are important models for children.

Conclusion

The importance of establishing secure but flexible foundations for learning, and ensuring that children can absorb new information, knowledge and skills effectively, is argued throughout this book. The approach is based on principle as well as theory and has been commended by government for the aptly named Foundation Stage. The key to adding new understanding to existing knowledge is to start where the learners are, to ask questions rather than to pass on answers directly, and to provide support rather than instruction. In this way, adults can help children to understand and appreciate challenges and to go beyond what they already know to find solutions. Now is the time to apply this thinking in practice and to establish the necessary connections which will support adventurous intellectual growth for all young children, and for those who have the privilege of living and working with them.

SIX

Assessing what matters in the early years

☐ **TONY BERTRAM AND CHRISTINE PASCAL**

Introduction

It is now widely accepted that the first five or six years of a child's life are probably the most critical in determining an individual's life chances. Long-term attitudes and deep-seated pathways of thinking are laid down in this critical period. Those who create and control learning and development in the early years are involved in fundamental processes which will affect children's expectations and achievements. What we choose to assess and test will impact on individual children's views of themselves as empowered and successful learners.

Laying the foundations on which a child's life edifice is to be built is a complex, skilful and very responsible task. It requires the builders to understand the importance of establishing robust footings in those areas that are going to stand the test of time, withhold the stresses of a lifetime and provide stability for further construction. How, and what, we should build early on to ensure a strong and enduring structure are key questions for early childhood educators because their work has a long-term and formative timescale. Those involved in early childhood education and care should never forget that their role is both as co-constructor and advocate of the empowered and effective learner.

We are currently going through a revolution in our understanding of how effective early learning is constructed and what factors contribute to lifelong achievement (Ball 1994; Bruner 1996; Bertram and Pascal 1999a). This knowledge has shaken the foundations of much of current educational practice. In recent years there has been an increasing emphasis on getting children into compulsory schooling early, focusing on the 'core skills' of literacy and numeracy, assessing narrowly and rigidly and, increasingly, promoting a formal and adult-led pedagogy. Although, in part this has been due to recognition of the importance of early learning for later achievement, the plan has been fatally flawed. It may even have contributed to a lifetime of underachievement for many children as they grow towards maturity.

The introduction of targets, indicators, outputs and outcomes is part of the UK government's understandable and well-meaning attempt to raise standards. But accountability has driven practitioners and politicians to seek easy answers to complex questions. In this attempt to raise standards, the standards have become more and more limited by what is most simply measurable.

But what is easily measurable cannot reflect the immense complexity of early learning. Practitioners have known this, but been faced with increasing demands to assess skills and knowledge which do not give a true reflection of the empowered and competent learner. Mercifully, there has begun a reassessment of what constitutes effective early learning, and an alternative curriculum, embodied in the Foundation Stage curriculum guidance (QCA 2000), is now being promoted. Yet there still remain, in the English educational system, critical anomalies between the philosophy and practices incorporated into the Foundation Stage documentation and those, for example, which characterize the literacy strategy. This is particularly true for those children in school reception classes where confusion and concern reigns about what is required of teachers of 4- and 5-year-olds. Even within DfES and its ancillary quangos, the QCA and Ofsted, there appears to be a difference of opinion between early years specialists in each division and their bureaucratic managers. Informed observers from abroad find it astonishing that young children should be subject to such didactic regimes (Bertram and Pascal 2000) when currently so much is being discovered about the ways in which young children learn and about the ways they see themselves as learners.

Critical in this is the impact on the curriculum of what and how we test and assess young children's abilities and competencies.

What do we need to know about young learners that will give us confidence that they are being assessed in ways that will empower them as learners for life?

Testing

It is imperative to begin with the assertion that the testing of young children will not give the evidence necessary either to make adequate judgements about what children already know and can do, or to give sufficient information for planning what they need to know next (Fisher 1998).

Testing is by definition someone else's judgement on a narrow range of indicators devised by a different person about what a third person (or people) have deemed to matter. The current national tests at the end of Key Stage 1 are a prime example of the inadequacies of testing. A judgement is made by a range of practitioners which can neither give confidence about validity or reliability. The indicators have been decided by those who believe knowledge and understanding of a narrow range of aspects of literacy and numeracy to be sufficient judgement about every child's current ability. Those who believe that there are different aims and purposes of early education and that the kind of learners we want to develop are critical, active citizens who can promote democracy and equity in their communities will find no evidence here.

Assessment regimes are not politically neutral but, rather, politically manipulative and ultimately coercive because they determine a child's long-term ability to make and shape the world in which they live. As Freire (1985) argued, education that pretends to be neutral and does not encourage critical, competent and questioning learners supports the dominant ideology in society. It also ultimately suppresses achievement and attainment for many groups of children – the very goals it professes to promote.

How young children learn

Research from a variety of disciplines is providing us with rich and powerful evidence about how children learn; the nature of such learning; and the ways in which early experiences shape the pattern of progress, achievement and fulfilment, throughout an individual's life. The research highlights the importance of, for example, dispositions to learning (Katz 1995); mastery orientation (Heyman *et al.* 1992); conflict resolution (Lantieri 1990); multiple intelligences (Gardner 1993); involvement, linkedness, emotional well-being and emotional literacy (Laevers and Van Santen 1995; Goleman 1996; Laevers 1996). As Sir Christopher Ball pointed out in the influential *Start Right* report (Ball 1994),

> Modern educational research is on the threshold of a revolution. The findings of brain science, for example, or the theory of multiple intelligence, or the idea of different styles of learning, or the recognition that people can learn to learn faster, are all pointing the way towards a new and powerful theory of learning which will be able to satisfy the three tests of explanation, prediction and aspiration. Central to the new theory will be a clearer understanding of learning development, and the sequence whereby people progress from infancy to become mature learners. In the (recent) past the professionalism of teachers has often been thought to reside in mastering the subject or discipline. But these are merely the tokens of learning. The art of learning (learning how to learn) is also concerned with the types, or 'super skills' and attitudes, of learning – of which motivation, socialisation and confidence are the most important. These are the fruits of successful early learning.
>
> (Ball 1994: para. 2.17)

National reports (National Commission on Education 1993; Ball 1994; House of Commons Select Committee Report 2000) have also indicated the importance of positive attributes towards early learning for lifelong achievement. They suggest that important learning characteristics associated with later achievement, such as aspiration, pro-socialization, self-esteem, motivation and confidence are established in the early years. These enabling attitudes have been called the 'super skills' of learning (Ball 1994).

While we recognize the importance of skills and knowledge in early learning, we believe that such a simplistic focus should not be the sole view of the early years curricula. We need to widen our perspective on 'outcomes' in early childhood and strengthen the practitioners' ability to support and assess those other areas of children's development that may be equally crucial to long-term success.

Study of early childhood learning needs to acknowledge the recent neuro-psychological research on brain growth in infants (summarized in Trevarthan 1992 and Phillips 1995) that supports the view that environments for young children that are staffed by caring, responsive and dependable adults are critical in the development of these attributes and dispositions in children. We believe there is a need to develop the ability of practitioners to support the child's learning in sensitive, stimulating and empowering ways (Bertram 1996). To sustain development in young minds, practitioners must be prepared to look at wider outcomes than academic knowledge and skills, and include dispositions to learn, social competence and emotional well-being, in their aspirations and intentions for young children. Developing practitioners' awareness of these important aspects of children's learning, and providing them with the means to assess and enhance them, will be a major challenge in developing a nation of lifelong learners.

A report by the influential US National Center for Clinical Infant Programs (Brazelton 1992) suggests that academic success rests predominantly on a child's early knowledge of how to learn, as well as what is learned. Goleman (1996) claims

> that school success is not predicted by a child's fund of facts or a precocious ability to read so much as by emotional and social measures; being self assured and interested; knowing what kind of behaviour is expected and how to rein in impulse to misbehave; being able to wait, to follow directions, and to turn to adults and peers for help; expressing needs whilst getting along with other children.
>
> (Goleman 1996: 193)

Our interest is targeted at birth to 6-year-olds because there is evidence to show that this is the critically important phase for establishing learning attitudes. Gender and race studies (Siraj-Blatchford 1996) show that lifelong attitudes are set early. Attitudes to 'self as a learner' follow the same pattern. Goleman (1996) talks of a 'window of opportunity' analogous to Lorenz's (1946) notion of 'imprinting'. These studies show that there is a biologically determined period when it is crucial to establish certain semi-permanent attitudes about learning. The stronger these are embedded, the greater their resilience to inevitable, climatic periods of poor stimulation, and the more likely that they will persist. The importance of this early period of social consciousness to lifelong achievement is recognized by Donaldson *et al.* (1983), who state that early childhood is

. . . a period of momentous significance for all people growing up in our culture. By the time this period is over, children will have formed conceptions of themselves as social
beings, as thinkers, and as language users, and they will
have reached certain important decisions about their own
abilities and their own worth.

(Donaldson *et al.* 1983: 1)

Measuring what is worthwhile

We live in an audited society where that which is measurable is
seen as significant. We need to ensure that what we are measuring truly matters and that we are not simply focusing on those
things that are easily measured. We need to be aware that a
focus on simplistic outputs for literacy and numeracy may impact on deeper and more important attitudes to learning. Hospital administrators, for example and as analogy, faced with targets
to reduce waiting lists, increased the throughput of minor sur-
gery cases rather than the more needy, long-term chronic and
difficult cases. Similarly, administrators faced with numerical indicators of measuring success, found ways of preventing people
from getting on the waiting list in the first place in order to meet
their targets. Parallels in education in the narrowing of the curriculum and in the exclusion of children with special needs make
the point that target setting needs to be treated cautiously.

The effective learner

The effective learner is a child who can sustain their ability to
explore the world in an open, critical, creative and joyful way in
order to extend their knowledge and understanding. Central to
this ability is a sense of empowerment. The learner who feels
empowered is able to function effectively within a social community and is also capable of acting upon and within that community with sensitivity and a sense of belonging. This sense of
agency and empowerment frees the child's exploratory drive and
allows their natural curiosity to emerge. They will also have a
sense of participation and influence upon their world, which
motivates them to engage in a socially constructive, inclusive and
equitable way. They will have the social and emotional skills
and competencies to engage with others, access opportunities

and express their needs as they take their learning forward. In short, the effective learner:

- is empowered and operates as a subject, not an object;
- has a sense of instrumentality and causality;
- is able to assert and articulate her sense of self and self-direction in relation to others;
- acts on her own behalf, and her actions come from her sense of self and self-will;
- takes her own decisions in relation to her life;
- is able to take, and enjoys taking, responsibility for herself, her decisions and her actions;
- has a sense of belonging and interconnectedness;
- is able to negotiate authority;
- has empathy and operates in reciprocity with others;
- has autonomy within the boundaries of accountability.

Through our work with practitioners and our understanding of the current professional and research literature on effective learning we have been able to identify three core constituent elements of the effective learner:

- dispositions to learn;
- social competence and self-concept;
- emotional well-being.

It is our thesis that it is these skills, attitudes and dispositions that should form the foundations of our assessment of young children's capabilities, for it is based on these domains that children become effective learners for life.

Dispositions to learn

Dispositions are the first key element to be identified in an effective learner and may be defined as behavioural characteristics and attitudes, exhibited frequently in young children and in the absence of external coercion, threat or reward, which indicate internalized habits of mind under conscious and voluntary control. Dispositions can be positive or negative. Educative dispositions are seen as positive when these behavioural characteristics are intentionally oriented to achieving broader goals than specific curriculum knowledge. Positive educative dispositions, which have long-term effects on lifelong learning, include independence, creativity, self-motivation and resilience. Dispositions are environmentally sensitive. They are acquired from and affected by interactive experiences with the environment, significant adults and peers. Unlike genetic predispositions, dispositions are not fixed at birth but are dynamic. Positive dispositions are learnt but they are rarely acquired didactically. These dispositions are central not only to educational achievement but to personal fulfilment.

Research in this area is developing fast and there is increasing evidence from the United States and from cross-national studies that these learning orientations and abilities, or dispositions, are evident in very young learners (aged 3 and 4 years) and continue to shape a child's progress and attitudes towards learning throughout their schooling and beyond. For example, Resnick (1987) shows that dispositions to learn are acquired early by children and are an important part of a child's motivation to explore the world. She also found that they were relatively long-lasting. For the past 15 years the American psychologists Dweck, Elliott and Leggett have been exploring academic motivation, learning characteristics and attitudes in children from the ages of 3 and 4 (Dweck and Leggett 1988; Elliot and Dweck 1988). Their scores of experiments have demonstrated that most children fall somewhere on a continuum of 'helplessness' to 'mastery' in their approach to learning. They found that children with a 'mastery' orientation to learning manage to coordinate their performance and learning goals successfully and set in motion cognitive and social processes which facilitate educational and social progress in the long term.

Assessing dispositions to learn

These are the indicators which we believe should be assessed if practitioners are to know whether children are developing positive attitudes towards learning and being a learner:

1 *Independence*: A disposition towards independence is revealed by a child's ability to be self-sufficient, to self-organize and self-manage. The independent child is as comfortable in exercising choice as she is in taking responsibility for her decisions and actions and their consequences. Independently disposed children enjoy opportunities for autonomy and choice making. They are strong enough to ask for support when required from adults or their peers, to ask questions and to negotiate opportunities for choice. They can be assertive when needed but

without resort to threat or dominance. Independently oriented children are capable of making selections and of locating and using resources appropriately. They develop competencies in organizing their environment, including the human environment, which allow them to have agency and affect change.

2 *Creativity*: A disposition towards creativity is characterized by those children who show curiosity and interest in their world, revelling especially in serendipity and originality. Such children enjoy exploring their environment, looking for patterns of meaning and comparing similarity and difference. The creative child is imaginative, spontaneous and innovative. They instigate and expand play ideas. They are secure enough in their immediate world to venture forth to explore new boundaries especially within the exciting zone of proximate development. They enjoy developing and extending their knowledge and thinking. They are rarely timid or fearful but have a confidence which allows them to embrace the undiscovered with enthusiasm, boldness and wonder. They can think laterally, innovatively and reflectively. Their confidence, originality and creativity are often expressed through humour. Satisfaction and reward from their exploration allows them to feel comfortable with the original and the different. Internally strongly located with an established self-identity based on secure notions of belonging, they can take risks and have satisfying adventures and face their world openly.

3 *Self-motivation*: A disposition towards self-motivation allows children, independently, to become deeply involved and engrossed in activities and challenges. Characteristically, they have plenty of self-initiated purposes, plans and objectives. They often will declare aims and goals and the intention to achieve them. Highly self-motivated children appreciate effort as a strategy and they show determination, persistence and precision. These well-motivated children are self-driven towards achieving their goals and the energy of their exploratory drive will be apparent. They also understand that mastery is a continual process of trial, error and adjustment. They see 'failure' as a temporary state, simply an intermediate part of the learning process and certainly not an indication of any fundamental and continuing personal inadequacy. They develop positive mindsets, such as: 'let's try', 'have a go' and 'can do'. They are smilingly keen to display newly acquired knowledge and skills, 'watch me', 'look at this' and 'did you know?' These children will self-manage, develop self-efficacy, and make choices to achieve their goals.

4 *Resilience*: A resilient child has the disposition to bounce back after setback, hindrance or frustration and retain temperament, personality and spirit. Such children develop a varied range of strategies for coping with change, recovering quickly and rebounding from disappointments. They are usually confident with an internal locus of control. Their resilience makes them happy with new challenges and often keen to try to tackle problems themselves. Although they appreciate the need for boundaries and structures, when routines are altered they are flexible and remain secure. They will sometimes develop self-survival mechanisms which allow them to vary their dependence on significant others without losing the bond. When reprimanded, they can separate errant behaviour from personal identity. They appreciate their right and that of others to have a different opinion. They understand the rewards to be gained from the processes of engagement, negotiation, assertion and persuasion. They understand that usually authority is logical but they are strong enough to know that sometimes adults get things wrong and, temporarily, that is something with which you may have to live. They understand that, in endeavour, setbacks are inevitable but they also know that there are limits to the extent one should strive without reward. They appreciate that sometimes it is reasonable to persist and sometimes it is reasonable to quit, sometimes you need to stand up and shout out and sometimes you need to be quiet and give way. They have strategies for conflict resolution.

Social competence and self-concept

Social competence is the second core element of the effective learner and may be defined as the ability of the child to reach out to others and to make connections and relationships that help them to survive and thrive. These competencies provide the child with the mechanisms to interact and interrelate with their community, a precondition for successful social living. The need for interdependency, a moral conscience and inner discipline are central to participation within a social network. A further precondition for developing effective relationships is that of self-concept, which provides the child with a strong sense of their own identity or worth. Self-esteem provides the child with the inner confidence to reach out and explore the unknown and forms a base from which they will form respectful relationships with others. These competencies are critical for learning which is essentially a social process.

It is now a well-established tenet in the field of cultural, social and neurological psychology that, from birth, learning is a process which occurs in a social context. The experiences and interactions of a child with others create internalized perceptions of self which then become predictors of their future behaviour. The child's main carer has a particularly strong influence in establishing respect for self and in empowering children to be strong (Whalley 1996). Practitioners need to work with parents and carers to create the development of children's self-respect and a strong self-esteem (Roberts 1996).

As with respect for self, young children also need to develop a respect for others. Lipman's pioneering work (1989) on the importance of respect for self and respect for others in young children aged 6 has demonstrated how programmes which develop these attributes directly benefit a child's cognitive and social development and educational progress. Such children are more likely to be able to acknowledge that there are alternative views held by others which are equally valid and should be given respect. This understanding of multiple perspectives has been shown to reduce classroom tensions and advance learning achievements. Gardner's groundbreaking work on multiple intelligences (1993) has shown that children with the same IQ can differ significantly in terms of school performance and he attributes this to differences in the children's inter- and intra-personal intelligence. This work has been followed up by Salovey and Mayer (1990) who have developed the concept of 'emotional intelligence', suggesting that it is more significant than IQ in determining an individual's life chances.

Assessing children's social competencies

We have identified five social competences which characterize the effective learner and which need to be assessed if children's skills in this important domain are to be extended:

1 *Establishing effective relationships*: A key social competence is the ability of the child to establish effective relationships with other children and adults. These relationships are crucial to the child's survival and healthy development. It requires the child to have the ability to initiate interactions, to cooperate with others, to accept others' ideas and suggestions and to

share experiences. The ability to make strong and close friendships with more than one person signals a child's connectedness
and interdependency, and will support their place within a
learning community.

2 *Empathy*: The ability to empathize is a social competence by
which the child can understand the world from another's
perspective. This is required for developing social relationships
and cooperating within collaborative group learning situations.
The empathetic child behaves considerately towards others
and shows respect for other people, their feelings and intentions. A sensitivity to the social context in which they are
operating and the effect this context has on themselves and
others is reflected in the child's actions and responses.

3 *Taking responsibility*: The ability of the child to take responsibility for their own thoughts, intentions and actions is a core
social competence for successful learning. This competence is
an essential determinant of effective social functioning. This
indicates the child's developing sense of right and wrong and
awareness of appropriate behavioural expectations; they will
have a moral self and an inner discipline. The child's actions
show a strong internal locus of control along with an ability
to treat others with respect, care and concern.

4 *Assertiveness*: The ability of the child to be assertive is a social
competence that provides them with the capacity to influence
and shape their learning and their lives. This gives the child
the capacity to make and carry through decisions and to have
a sense of themselves as active and valued members of a community of learners. The assertive child will communicate and
voice their opinions and ideas, offer suggestions and negotiate. They will question and be inquisitive but listen to others'
opinions and suggestions. This will be reflected in their interactions which will be without aggression or undue deference
or evasiveness.

5 *Awareness of self*: A key precondition for effective social interaction is the child's developing sense of self and self-worth in
relation to their personality, their family, their home and their
culture. This competence is reflected in their understanding of
their own personal identity and sense of belonging. The child
with self-worth will have a positive self-image and demonstrate self-esteem. They will show a sense of control over their
decisions and rights and have pride in their achievements.
They will also have a developing capacity to reflect upon their
sense of self in relation to the world.

Emotional well-being

Emotional well-being is the third core element of the effective learner and focuses on the child's ability to feel comfortable with themselves. This is demonstrated in their displaying an open, receptive attitude to the environment. This enables them to be assertive and to show and manage their emotions. They will also reflect peace, vitality and zeal for life and will enjoy participating without too much anxiety. Such qualities are seen to be critical in sustaining learning in the long term and to sustain them through difficulties and learning challenges.

The growing number of children with psychological and emotional difficulties in many developed countries has been shown to be a major factor in increasing underachievement and school dropout (Achenbach and Howell 1989; Thomas *et al.* 1989; Goleman 1996). Examples of studies which demonstrate the link between 'well-being' and educational performance include Salovey and Mayer (1990) who found that children with 'ego resilience' or emotional well-being are more likely to be self-regulating, adaptive, to control impulses, to have a sense of self-efficacy and to operate in a social environment.

Laevers (1996) describes young children as readily displaying the level of their 'well-being' in eight observable signals. Children with high levels of well-being are, he says 'like fish in water' in their educational environments and maximize their learning potential. The New Zealand Early Childhood Curriculum 'Te Whiriki' (New Zealand Ministry of Education 1996) uses the strand of 'well-being' as a permeation issue which interweaves with their curriculum principles. Well-being leads to the establishment of the confidence to explore, and the foundation of remembered and anticipated places and experiences. It encourages the positive development of that innate exploratory drive that characterizes humans. Above all, children who display the quality of well-being have learnt the joy of empowering contact with responsive people.

Assessing emotional well-being

There appear to be four elements of emotional well-being that characterize the effective learner and which should be assessed to support children in the development of this crucial domain:

1 *Emotional literacy*: A key element of emotional well-being is the ability of the child to be emotionally literate. This reflects

their fluency in both feeling and expressing their emotions and being able to pass through a range of feelings towards a sense of equilibrium. The emotionally literate child is aware of their emotions and is able to articulate and express them. The child shows self-control and is able to manage a range of emotions. They are able to be self-motivated and persist in the face of adversity. They show the ability to empathize with others and have a growing understanding of the effect of their actions on others. The fundamental influence of emotions on learning and on the child's ability to free their exploratory drive is often underestimated.

2 *Empowerment*: The empowered child has an inner strength and robust self-will which encourages self-direction and self-management of new learning. They have a strong sense of self-worth, identity and confidence. The child feels able to trust and is able to determine her own actions, appreciate the consequences of these actions and make choices. An empowered child can cope with changes in their life and has a sense of self-value, knowing that their emotional needs will be met, being unafraid to ask for support when required.

3 *Connectedness*: A further precondition for emotional well-being is that of connectedness. To learn effectively the child requires an ability to relate to others, to interlink events and situations in their life and feel a part of the whole. They also need to have a sense of attachment and belonging to the people with whom they come into close and regular contact, both adults and children. The community in which the child operates provides the context in which they feel their sense of value and within which they are able to participate. The connected child will have a working knowledge of the pattern of their day-to-day lives, and how things function, and will feel able to contribute to and shape this.

4 *Positive self-esteem*: A major contributing factor to emotional well-being is positive self-esteem. This indicates the child's sense of self-worth and personal identity and the way in which this is perceived by the community of adults and children within which they operate. Self-esteem is shaped first by the experiences of the child in relation to others, but reflects their own perception of self and the value that they believe this self is given in relation to others. The child with positive self-esteem feels capable, significant and worthy but not necessarily perfect, and does not feel the need to strive for perfection. Positive self-esteem allows the child to have a realistic appraisal

of self and to deal with their feelings, both positive and negative, in relation to risk, success and failure. These are key skills for the effective learner.

Conclusion

This chapter has sought to set an alternative agenda for the assessment of young children. Our intention is to move beyond the narrow focus on literacy and numeracy and study, more rigorously, the dispositions, social skills and emotional development of young learners. We believe that these lay the foundations for the quality of learning that is to follow. If judgements are made about young children, based on their knowledge and memory of certain limited skills and facts, then we may relegate them to a lifetime of underachievement. If we enhance their attitudes and dispositions to continue to learn, then we will have given them the foundations to be learners for life.

As Ball (1994: para. 2.17) points out, 'modern educational research is on the threshold of a revolution', a view echoed by Bruner (1996), who talks of a 'cognitive revolution' which is changing the way we think about learning. The knowledge base which supports our understanding of early learning is developing fast, and clearly showing that a focus on education as the injection of facts, subjects and disciplines of knowledge alone, particularly in the early years, provides only a partial explanation of what makes for effective and lifelong learning. Our focus on defining and describing the effective learner has two main purposes. First, we are attempting to encourage those who work with young children to apply this new knowledge to their practice and ensure their work is at the forefront of professional knowledge. Second, we are aiming to communicate this newly acquired professional knowledge to those who create policy so that they also may act from an informed base.

There is an urgent need to develop robust methods for assessing those other elements of early learning which appear to be critical in ensuring the child progresses as a lifelong learner. Currently, the aspects of learning which form the basis of the national testing regime fail to capture the critical determinants of success and so fail as predictors of longer term strength. In challenging the current testing agenda we should aim for the knowledge revolution in early learning to come off the shelves and feed directly into the actions of those who shape children's early educational lives.

SEVEN

The consequences of inadequate investment in the early years

☐ GILLIAN PUGH

Introduction

After years of neglect, the twin concepts of prevention and early intervention have at last begun to gain acceptance. Policy decisions within central government over the past five years have recognized that many of the problems experienced by teenagers and young adults could have been prevented or at least ameliorated had there been a greater investment in appropriate support at an earlier stage. To those who work with families with young children, this seems so obvious as to be hardly worth arguing for, but for politicians it has taken rather longer to recognize.

This chapter will draw on a wide range of research evidence to explore the factors which put some children and young people at risk of being socially excluded, and will examine ways in which some of those risks can be avoided or reversed. It will look at the costs of failing to intervene early in children's lives and will examine the concept of resilience, or those attributes or factors which can give children the capacity to withstand the challenges and threats of life and to 'bounce back' from potential setbacks. And it will argue that high-quality early education and effective support for parents can both play a key part in providing children with the resilience they need to develop to their full potential.

Raymond: a case study

But first, let us meet Raymond, a young person who graduated
last year from the education service run by Coram Family's Leaving Care Service.

Raymond has been in local authority care since he was a baby.
Although there were periods when he returned to live with his
mother, he has spent most of his life in children's homes. While
in foster care, Raymond started primary school. However, his behaviour became very challenging due to frequent changes in his
life and he was excluded and referred to a children's home with
an education unit. Although Raymond remained at the children's
home, his behaviour continued to be a problem, both within the
home itself and within the education unit.

When Raymond reached secondary school age, he resumed
contact with his mother and went to stay with her. He was re-
introduced to mainstream education when he started at a boy's
secondary school, but he was excluded before the end of the first
academic year. Raymond was a persistent non-attender and again
displayed serious behavioural problems at school and at home.
Over the next two years, he attended three children's homes, all
with the education units.

When he was 13 Raymond returned to his mother's home, where
he stayed for over a year. He did not attend school during this
time, nor did he receive any alternative education. At 14 he was
placed with foster carers until he was 16. He did not receive any
education during this time.

At this point social services referred Raymond to the Education
Service run by Coram Family's Leaving Care Service. They were concerned that he had come to the end of his secondary education
without any qualifications, few basic skills and few job prospects.

His disruptive early life and his experience in the care system
had resulted in an inconsistent and discordant educational background. Raymond had very clearly 'missed out' on some of the
fundamental necessary skills required for academic developments:
for example he had great difficulty spelling all but fairly simple
words, as well as difficulty with days of the week and months of
the year. He was also unfamiliar with basic rules of grammar and
punctuation.

When Raymond started classes at Coram's Education Service
there was some initial reluctance to learn. But staff worked very
hard to motivate Raymond and raise his self-confidence. Raymond
responded positively to the non-competitive and informal learning environment. He was encouraged to focus on his strengths,
particularly his flair for mathematics and his creative talents. By
the end of the first term, Raymond was beginning to be aware of

his own abilities and recognized his own potential to do well. This was a crucial factor in serving to enthuse and motivate him. Raymond realized that if he worked hard enough and was ambitious enough he could fulfil his dream to be an electrician.

A year later Raymond left the Education Service with Achievement Tests in numeracy and literacy and he is now employed as an electrician and taking a Modern Apprenticeship.

This is a story with a happy ending – but the majority of children whose early lives are disrupted are not so lucky.

The beginning of a new century provided an opportunity to reflect on how well we as a society were treating our children and young people. How many young people were reaching adulthood as self-sufficient, confident and socially responsible individuals? What support were they finding from their families and from society more generally? And how many children had experiences similar to Raymond's?

Children and families: a view at the millennium

A review of children and families at the millennium (Pugh 1999) concluded that while children were living longer and healthier lives and were better educated than their parents, there was a level of unease and uncertainty surrounding children's lives and a concern about their social and emotional well-being. The review found that children were increasingly restricted in the amount of freedom that they could enjoy: they were unable to play independently or even walk or cycle to school, largely due to increased traffic on the roads, and fear of stranger danger. It was noted that, with the increasing emphasis within the education system on raising standards, there were few opportunities for creativity and imagination, and too much control on how children's time was spent.

The review also pointed to the level of stress experienced by many children – whether through the increasingly high rates of family breakdown, the high levels of unemployment, or pressures within the education system and the regime of constant testing. It is not perhaps surprising that an estimated one in five children experience mental health problems and that one in ten have problems that are sufficiently disabling to stop them doing everyday things such as going to school, making friends etc.

(Mental Health Foundation 1999). But above all, the review noted the very high level of poverty, with one in three children (over four million) now living on or below the poverty line.

Many of the likely outcomes of being born into poverty have been reported in Chapters 3 and 4, but there is now an extensive literature which points to the cumulative nature of disadvantage which puts some children at greater risk of social exclusion than others. Studies of children's health and of educational attainment consistently show that social class and income levels continue to have a dramatic effect on outcomes for children. Children in low-income families are more prone to accidents, acute infections, respiratory diseases and lack of psychological well-being. They are also less likely to do well at school. The Department of Health estimates that each year some 3 per cent of children – that would be approximately 350,000 – are living in an environment of 'low warmth and high criticism' (Department of Health 1995), and 160,000 are referred to the child protection process. Of these, over half are from families lacking a wage earner. Studies of children such as Raymond show that poverty is a major factor among those who are taken into the care system to be 'looked after' by local authorities. The majority of children coming into care are living with only one parent, their families receive income support, more than half live in poor neighbourhoods, and there is a high incidence of crowded accommodation (Bebbington and Miles 1989).

The cost of support services

The cost of all this misery is considerable, in both human and financial terms. A recent review by Coram Family of support services for children causing concern in primary schools pointed to the growing number of children who are clingy and despondent; unresponsive and withdrawn; unable to concentrate or cope with or respond to new instructions; afraid to try anything new. Sometimes, though not always, teachers knew why: disruption at home through parents separating or divorcing, new partners or new siblings; the physical or mental ill health of parents; the stress of poverty or employment; or domestic violence (Ball in press). Children who do not acquire the basic skills of literacy or numeracy in primary school, for all of these reasons, are likely to perform poorly in secondary school, to leave school early without qualifications, to have problems in accessing the labour market, and associated problems related to drug and alcohol abuse, criminal behaviour and mental and physical health problems. There is a rise in the number of exclusions from primary schools, and increasing numbers of children are registered as having emotional and behavioural difficulties and are being treated for psychoses, severe depression and eating disorders. Emotions and learning cannot be separated. Anxiety inhibits curiosity, and how children feel about themselves impacts on how they learn (Hartley Brewer 1999). Positive early investment in the lives of all of these children would have been cheaper than the costs of dealing with the consequences.

The potential of prevention and early intervention in children's lives is now well understood. Simple, relatively inexpensive measures, put into effect early, can save the need for more complex interventions later on: a fence at the top of the cliff is infinitely preferable to an ambulance at the bottom (Sinclair *et al.* 1997; Little and Mount 1999). As Paul Boateng MP, Minister for Children, said in launching the Children's Fund in 2000,

> If in childhood all too often obvious early signs of trouble are missed, children can go on to experience very serious problems and crises that have to be tackled through costly interventions when it is too late to avoid lasting disadvantage. They enter childhood with little hope of a decent job or being able to play a fulfilled role in society.

Prevention

Prevention is usually described in three stages. Primary prevention describes interventions made before problems have manifest themselves, and are often targeted at whole populations, such as immunization, or an early education programme. Secondary prevention implies that a problem has already become apparent and action is needed to prevent this becoming more serious, for example the reading recovery programme described later in this chapter. When problems are multiple, complex or long-standing, tertiary level prevention will be required, for example referral to the child protection register to prevent the child being removed from the family.

A wide range of studies have attempted to identify measures which could prevent family breakdown, poor health, developmental delay, childhood accidents, child abuse, low educational attainment, truancy or exclusion from school, juvenile offending, mental health problems, substance misuse, and early unwanted pregnancy. What becomes clear is the interconnection between these areas, and the overlap both in the factors which put children at risk and those factors which might protect them. It is important to stress that risk factors are often multiplicative. Werner and Smith (reported in Carnegie 1994) found that when children showed only one risk factor for social and academic difficulties, their outcomes were no worse than those of children with no risk factors. But when children had two or more risk factors, they were four times as likely to develop problems:

> Policy makers must recognise that it pays to help families increase protective factors in raising their youngest children. Enhancing parents' social supports, encouraging positive parenting practices, and stimulating the child's cognitive development all appear effective in enabling children to achieve a good start in life.
>
> (Carnegie 1994: 12)

All children are exposed to some risks, and how individual children perceive the risks and cope with the difficulties will depend on their particular disposition and circumstances. But importantly, risk factors are not predictors. A web of interrelated factors may indicate probabilities but not certainties, and we must be aware of false positives as well as false negatives. Early intervention may however shift the balance of probability, changing the distribution between good and bad outcomes to optimize the good and minimize the bad. There is also of course a considerable difference between reviewing the background of those with problems, and making predictions about who is likely to experience difficulties. This becomes clear if we look at the Cambridge study of juvenile delinquency, which followed 411 working-class boys from their eighth birthday into adulthood (West and Farrington 1982). A fifth of the boys were convicted as juveniles, and from this it was possible to predict those factors which were identified at 8 which best predicted delinquency – being troublesome at primary school, coming from a poor family, having a large family, having a criminal parent, being badly brought up and being of below average intelligence. But it is salutary to note that six out of ten primary school children with these characteristics will *not* become delinquent – we must beware of labelling children and creating self-fulfilling prophecies.

Risk and protective factors

With this caution in mind, the following charts summarizes the key risk factors that we know from research are most likely to have an adverse effect on children's development, separating them into factors inherent in the child, factors in the family (and particularly those related to styles of parenting), and broader community-based factors.

Against these risk factors are those protective factors that we know can help to develop the resilience that children will require if they are to thrive.

Risk factors	Protective factors
In the child	*In the child*
Low birthweight	Personal disposition
Hyperactivity, anti-social activity	Being female
Genetic influences	Easy temperament
Low intelligence	Secure attachment
Developmental delay	Ability to solve problems
Difficult temperament	Internal locus of control
Low self-esteem	High self-esteem, autonomy
Poor communicator	Good communicator

Some of these factors are not susceptible to intervention – we would not wish, for example, to interfere in the gender balance even though we know that boys are more susceptible to a wide range of risks than girls. But it is interesting to note those characteristics which have been found to be particularly important in creating resilience in children: the ability to solve problems, an internal locus of control, self-esteem and autonomy. I will return to these later in considering the role of early education in promoting resilience in young children. Secure attachment I will consider below.

Risk factors	Protective factors
In the family	*In the family*
Difficult or early pregnancy	Authoritative parenting
Poor physical or mental health	Warm and affectionate
Poor parenting	relationships
– poor supervision	Predictable and consistent
– erratic and inconsistent	Open and effective
discipline	communication

– low involvement with child	Time spent together
– high criticism, low warmth	Clear limit setting
Conflict between parents	Empathy
Criminal activity	Support for education

There is growing research knowledge about the different styles of parenting and the impact that these have on outcomes for children (Patterson 1982; West and Farrington 1982; Pugh *et al*. 1994). Positive, nurturing relationships between children and parents, and parents' ability to see the world through the eyes of their children or put themselves in their shoes, provide the crucial foundation for a secure and well-adjusted future. I return to the importance of parenting below.

Risk factors	**Protective factors**
In the community	*In the community*
Social isolation, lack of networks	Supportive networks
Poor schools	Good schools
– lack of early education	– with high expectations
– low reading age at 7	– good early education
– bullying, truancy, exclusion	– appropriate curriculum
Poor housing	Good housing
Poor neighbourhood	High standard of living
No leisure facilities	Good leisure facilities
Poor material circumstances	

For the purposes of this chapter, the community-based factor that is of most relevance is that of good schools, with high expectations of all their pupils, the access to high-quality early education, with an appropriate curriculum. I will return to this shortly.

Pulling these three groups of factors together, it is possible to summarize the key protective factors required by children if they are to thrive as

- an adequate standard of living;
- a temparament/disposition that encourages care giving, leading to high self-esteem, sociability and autonomy, the ability to solve problems, and an internal locus of control;
- dependable care givers, where children can grow up in a family with one or two caring adults, who have positive and appropriate child-rearing practices;
- networks of community support, including a pro-social peer group, high-quality early education, and schools where children are valued and learning is encouraged.

If we look back on the many children and young people who are currently at risk, through mental health problems, through exclusion from school, through lack of a stable family, it is possible to see in almost every child, as with Raymond, a thread which goes back to difficult experiences early in life. This must be the most effective time at which both to intervene, both in terms of personal health and happiness, and in terms of later costs.

The concept of resilience

Over the past two decades the concept of resilience has received increasing attention. In pulling together this wealth of research, it has become clear that if children are to develop to their full potential, then there are certain characteristics and attributes that will help them to 'bounce back' in a resilient way when the going gets rough. Resilience in a material is a property which enables it to resume its original shape after being stretched or bent. Resilient children have been described as having the capacity to get back in balance after being pushed out of it, to tolerate greater challenges without breaking down, and it has been noted that this is most easily acquired during infancy (Kraemer 1999). Others have described resilience as normal development in difficult circumstances, or the presence of emotional intelligence. Emotional intelligence is seen as a crucial factor in 'adult success' (see Goleman 1996) and it is possible to detect it in very young children. Emotional intelligence is also fundamental to the development of cognitive skills and the ability to come to terms with negative life events.

Resilience can be characterized by a number of attributes, some of which we have already seen above

- self-knowledge, self-esteem and self-confidence;
- the capacity to create and maintain friendships with peers and gain the support of adults;
- trust in and empathy with others;
- a sense that the child's world has a purpose and a design – something that many children in care do not feel, as they are moved around from one temporary family to another;
- a set of values and beliefs that structure the child's response to the world;

- an internal locus of control, a sense that the child can influence their circumstances;
- optimism and clear aspirations;
- reflectiveness and the capacity to solve problems.

If these are the characteristics of the resilient child, how can we support children to become resilient, to believe in themselves and in their capacity to make a difference to their own lives? The most important starting point, as we noted above, is the promotion of secure attachments with parent or parents in infancy, for without these it is difficult for children to begin to develop further relationships outside the immediate family as they start nursery and then go on to school. The second main challenge has to be the encouragement of competencies and problem-solving skills through a rich learning environment – and this is where high-quality early education comes in. Underpinning both of these is our growing understanding of the development of the brain during the first three years of life, and the effect of environmental influences on this development. Severe environmental stress has a negative effect not only on how the brain develops, but how it functions, and underlies our capacity to make and sustain relationships (Carnegie 1994). High self-esteem is associated with positive life experiences such as warm and caring relationships, and with positive reinforcement through success and achievement at school.

Promoting resilience through the family

The family is probably the most critical factor in promoting resilience in children, and in providing a secure yet stimulating environment for children as they grow up. The positive, nurturing relationships and the empathy that were so important in the protective factors noted above are well illustrated in the fascinating work of Colwyn Trevarthan, whose films of early interaction between parents and babies show the sensitive reciprocal give and take or 'dance' in which the infant leads and the parent responds. These relationships have their roots in secure attachments between parents and child in early infancy. Bowlby's work on the central importance of children's early attachment to their parents and one or two carers if they are to develop a secure sense of self and emotional equilibrium, has tended to be dismissed by those who have interpreted it as requiring mothers to stay at home full-time to care for their pre-school children. This was never Bowlby's intention, however, and attachment theory does make an important contribution to our growing understanding of the importance of social and emotional competence as the basis of self-esteem, and is a key ingredient in the concept of resilience. Children who are unable to form secure and dependable attachments to their parents – who find their parents cold or hostile, or lacking in empathy, or totally unpredictable in how they respond to them, perhaps due to depression or abuse of drugs or alcohol – will find it more difficult to form trusting relationships with their peers or with their future partners or, in time, with their own children.

Effective early education, which we will come to in a moment, also involves parents, and complements what is happening at home. The home as a learning environment, and the parent's role as educator, has long been recognized by good practitioners and confirmed by research findings. Evidence presented by the National Child Development Study (of 16,000 children born in one week in March 1958) to the Plowden committee on primary education provided a powerful reminder of the importance of parents. This study found that the variation in parental attitudes to their children's education can account for more of the variations in children's school achievement than either the variation in home circumstances or in the schools themselves (Davie *et al.* 1972). Later studies of the children who had everything stacked against them – children described in *Born to Fail* – but who 'escaped from disadvantage' and succeeded at school were those whose parents, and particularly their fathers, supported their education (Pilling 1991).

The NCDS research was published at about the same time that Uri Bronfenbrenner (1974) published his influential overview of US Headstart programmes, which concluded that strategies which included parents in early education were more effective in terms of long-term gains than those which did not. This is also a compelling message from the High/Scope research discussed below. While the high-quality curriculum is central to this programme's long-term effectiveness, so too is the involvement of parents, and their increased interest in and expectations of their children's education. Improved early performance, higher teacher expectation, increased pupil motivation and increased parental aspirations become mutually reinforcing.

Most recently the importance of the educational environment of the home has been highlighted by the EPPE project, which has found aspects of the home learning environment to have a significant impact on children's cognitive development at age 3 and again at school entry (Sylva *et al.* 2000).

The impact of the home is not always positive, however, as the study of children causing concern at primary school cited above makes clear. Children who misbehave or underachieve at school are often those who are troubled at home, and parental conflict has a clear impact on children's ability to concentrate in school (Hartley Brewer 1999).

For many parents, particularly those who were less successful at school and lack confidence in their abilities to support their children, the challenges may be considerable. A national study of parenting education and support (Pugh *et al.* 1994) showed how damaging it was to parents' confidence and to their capacity as educators if schools made them feel their role was unimportant or misguided – 'We don't like them to come to school reading', or 'We don't do capital letters yet'. Just as children can only learn if they feel secure, motivated and confident, so too parents must feel confident. The preliminary findings from the early excellence centres programme (Bertram and Pascal 1999b) echoes a considerable body of research which points to the value of open access family centres and early childhood centres in providing support to vulnerable families, and in enabling families to support each other (see Pugh *et al.* 1994; Making 1997; Wigfall and Moss in press). For the parents, these studies point to increased self-confidence, a greater understanding of how children develop and learn, enhanced parenting skills, reduction in family breakdown, decreased social isolation, more involvement in the local community, and increased take-up of training opportunities and adult education. All of this had a considerable knock-on effect on the children, included increased cognitive and social skills, and the important but difficult to quantify reduction in later more costly interventions. It was evidence such as this and the growing recognition of the importance of the first three years of life, which led to the establishment of the Sure Start programme.

Promoting resilience through early education: cost-effectiveness studies

The main evidence for the effectiveness of high-quality early education, and of its 'preventive' and 'protective' qualities, comes from the United States. Some of the earliest evidence is found in the meta-analysis of high-quality early intervention programmes undertaken by Lazar and Darlington (1982). Results showed that participation in excellent, cognitively orientated pre-school programmes was associated with later school competence and avoidance of assignment to special education. Interviews revealed that those who had participated in the programmes were more positive about their schooling and the parents revealed higher aspirations for the employment of their children. As Rutter (1985) has argued, 'The long-term educational benefits stem not from what children are specifically taught but from effects on children's attitudes to learning, on their self-esteem and on their task orientation'.

A further meta-analysis by Slavin and colleagues (1994) concluded that high-quality early childhood intervention was effective in preparing disadvantaged children for school entry. The more successful programmes combined several elements of intervention, lasted for a number of years, and involved intensive participation by children and families. He found that it was particularly important to carry out the intervention close to school entry, or to implement 'top-up' near to school entry.

The best known and most rigorous of the early intervention research is the Perry Pre-school Project, known as High/Scope, which has been evaluated over a period of 30 years (Schweinhart *et al.* 1993). The intervention, for 65 children who attended a half-day programme over two years, and a control group of 58 children who stayed at home, showed some significant results. The programme included a high-quality, well-structured curriculum, together with high levels of parent involvement and a home visting programme, delivered by well-trained teachers. The results, confirmed up to the age of 27, found higher levels of employment and high school graduation among those who attended the High/Scope programme, lower levels of arrests and anti-social behaviour, higher levels of home ownership and car ownership, lower levels of unwanted teenage pregnancies, and less recourse to social services or special educational provision. On the basis of this data, Schweinhart *et al.*'s cost–benefit analysis found that for every $1000 invested in the pre-school programme, at least $7160 had been saved by society. These calculations were based on the financial cost to society of juvenile delinquency, remedial education, income support and joblessness, set against the running costs of the programme. The economic analysis also estimates the return to society of taxes from the higher paid preschool graduates.

Other studies have also shown that the costs of early childhood programmes were more than offset by the savings later on in the children's schooling and medical care (Sylva and Evans 1999). The impact is particularly strong for children from disadvantaged backgrounds, a view supported by Ofsted (1993) who found that nursery education enhanced the ability of children to take advantage of and benefit from school, particularly those children whose social experiences are limited, who had limited vocabulary and restricted speech patterns.

There have been no longitudinal studies in the UK comparable to the High/Scope study in looking at the long-term effects of high-quality early education, although the ongoing EPPE study (Sylva *et al.*) is looking at the impact of a range of variables, including home background and type of pre-school centre, on outcomes for children. Cost savings are claimed in the preliminary findings of the evaluation of early excellence centres (Bertram and Pascal 1999b), although these early findings are not easy to substantiate. Nevertheless, on the basis of case studies of some eight centres, the authors claim that £1 invested in early education and support saves £8 on alternative services, for example special education, or more costly family support services.

An appropriate curriculum and pedagogy

It is important to note that it is only those pre-school programmes with a child-centred, play-based curriculum which encourages active learning and parental involvement which lead to these encouraging outcomes for children. Weikart and colleagues compared the effects of three different curricula – High/Scope, a 'free play' programme and a formal pre-school curriculum – and found that, while all three raised IQ levels at school entry, at the age of 15 children who had attended the formal programme engaged in more anti-social behaviour and had lower commitment to school than those involved in the other two programmes. The best outcomes were for those who engaged in the High/Scope programme (Schweinhart *et al.* 1986). This study has been replicated by Sylva and colleagues (Nabuco and Sylva 1996).

In pulling together these and other findings for the RSA Early Learning enquiry, Kathy Sylva adds these words to Rutter's remarks quoted above:

> Nearly a decade later we can put in place some of the pieces unavailable when Rutter wrote his classic review. The most

important impact of early education appears to be on children's aspirations, motivations and school commitment. These are moulded through experiences in the pre-school classroom which enable children to enter school with a positive outlook and begin a school career of commitment and social responsibility.

(Sylva 1994)

In her review, Sylva draws on the work of Dweck and others to explore the concept of a 'mastery' orientation towards learning, whereby children employ problem-solving strategies when confronted with difficulties or challenges. By comparison the 'helpless' children avoided challenge and gave up easily, with negative views of their own abilities and a low sense of self-worth. The helpless children were pursuing performance goals, whereas the mastery children were more focused on learning. Dweck and her colleagues argue that when children view intelligence as a malleable quality, and realize that effort will lead to increased intelligence, they tend to persist in the face of difficulty.

Sylva draws on the High/Scope curriculum, and its embodiment of Vygotsky's notion of effective instruction within the 'zone of proximal development' (Vygotsky 1962), to argue that a curriculum which develops a mastery or learning orientation is more effective, and suggests that the plan, do, review cycle is the cause of greater autonomy, commitment and aspirations – and thus the longer term effectiveness of the High/Scope programme. It is not of course only the High/Scope curriculum which encourages mastery in young children. Much high-quality nursery education in schools and nurseries across the UK provides exactly the kind of curriculum which recognizes and responds to children as active learners, and the *Curriculum Guidance for the Foundation Stage* (QCA 2000) is the first acknowledgement from government of the importance of this approach.

I believe we can go further than this, in linking the concept of mastery with the characteristics of resilience – the self-concept of the learner, the sense of control over one's learning, the ability to resolve conflicts and live in harmony with one's peers, and the problem-solving skills. High-quality early education can help children develop the skills for coping with difficulty and with failure, and help them to see that effort brings its own rewards. It supports children's personal, social and emotional well-being as well as their physical and cognitive development; it promotes positive attitudes and dispositions towards learning; and encourages children to persist with challenging tasks. Learning carries risks and the possibility of failure; it involves listening and concentrating, and being prepared to let go – all of which are difficult for children with trouble and uncertainty in their lives. The greater emotional literacy that comes with these mastery competencies and the growth of self-esteem that derives from them, the better will children be able to take advantage of what the education system – and life – has to offer them.

Conclusion

The four key protective factors that have been identified in this chapter if children are to thrive are an adequate standard of living, a temperament and disposition that leads to high self-esteem, dependable care givers, and high-quality early education. It is clear that early education alone cannot provide all the answers or prevent all the problems, and that support for parenting, and the enhancement of good relationships between parents and children, are absolutely essential. But high-quality early education can do much to create a sense of mastery and resilience in children, giving them confidence and with it high self-esteem. It can encourage in children a belief in their ability to deal with change and adapt where appropriate, it can give them a range of problem-solving skills and the ability to get on well with others. It provides the foundations upon which all future learning is built, and the disposition to learn and to succeed.

Conclusions: The foundations of learning

☐ JULIE FISHER

Fact 1: Foundations take longer to create than buildings

In early education we have for some time been subjected to a top-down pressure on our educational principles and practice. Too many people are overly concerned with educational outcomes without appreciating the necessity for appropriate educational processes. The current emphasis on target setting, test results, value-added data and narrowly defined academic success has led to a climate where these constitute the rationale for children's experiences once schooling begins.

But, as the authors in this book have so eloquently argued, at this stage effective education is not about height but about breadth and depth. It is not about finished buildings but about establishing the foundations upon which any future buildings might be securely constructed. Our task is to give children the underpinning – the understandings, the skills and above all the attitudes – to be learners for life.

Learning for young children is a never-ending quest to make sense of what is new, incomprehensible, fascinating and compelling and to make connections with what is already known and understood. And there are so many connections to make! Young children's limited life experiences mean that they need time to try things out, to raise questions, to get things wrong and to revisit emerging ideas. It is a time for wallowing in learning, not for rushing through it. There is a dichotomy here with the current notion of 'pace' as a desirable attribute of teaching. Pace often causes teachers to be intent on their own agenda rather than the children's, to cover the curriculum and its intended learning outcomes and to move children on – not because they are ready, but because otherwise they will fall behind their adult-driven targets.

When adults constantly drive the pace of teaching it can mean that golden opportunities for learning are missed. In *Hare Brain Tortoise Mind* (1997) Guy Claxton reminds us vividly that learning experiences that rely on slick answers to quick questions, that value explanation over observation and that operate with a sense of urgency and impatience, only develop one dimension of our human faculties. There are a multitude of ideas, thoughts and solutions which only come about if the unconscious realms of the mind are given time to dwell, to reflect, to consider and to muse. Learning, says Claxton (1997: 6), emerges from uncertainty, and learning environments need to tolerate this uncertainty, 'to act as a seed bed in which ideas germinate and responses form'.

Whatever life experiences and achievements are to be built on top of early learning, they need foundations that are rich, broad, varied and robust. Without the broad and deep foundations of a curriculum experience that provides learning opportunities across all aspects of the curriculum with equal rigour and commitment, then the edifice of 'achievement' will be all too temporary. The effects of high-quality early childhood education may not be readily seen, especially by the untrained eye. But if the foundations we lay are to be the bedrock for lifelong learning, then surely the wait is worthwhile.

Fact 2: The higher the building, the firmer the foundations have to be

The notion of 'height' in education is difficult to conceptualize. Perhaps the nearest equation is with 'success'. But does success mean achieving Level 3 in Key Stage 1 tests; 5 A–Cs at GCSE; your 25 metre swimming certificate or a badge for growing a prize marrow at the horticultural fair? There is a danger in our current educational climate that achievement is equated with whatever it is that tests and examinations measure. If it can be given a level, a label or a competency then it is recognized and deemed to be worthwhile.

But human achievement is so much more varied and infinitely more rich. If all that we value about a young child's phenomenal range of skills and understandings is that he or she 'can recognize five letter shapes by shape and sound' or 'can describe size' (SCAA 1997) then many children are doomed to failure at a very early age and may never gain the self-esteem to discover their real potential. More than that, we as a society would lose the very lifeblood of those who are creatively, musically and interpersonally gifted, without necessarily being intellectually inclined. Of course, if we adopt Howard Gardner's thesis (1993), then these talents are intelligences in themselves. Who is to say that being able to pass an IQ test makes one more or less able, more or less valuable, than being able to achieve in the domains of physical or creative prowess?

A further danger for the early years is that far too many policy makers and politicians mistakenly believe that in order to achieve certain standards at age 7 or 14, children must begin to rehearse the same skills at the earliest possible age. To begin with, early education is more important than this. It is important in its own right and not just as a preparation for what is to come. The Foundation Stage has rightly introduced this period of learning as a distinct phase (QCA 2000) and early education should never again be viewed as merely the precursor of something else. What children experience now will indeed affect what is to follow, but if those experiences are inappropriate – too difficult, irrelevant or disconnected from the needs and interests of the developing young learner – then all future development is in jeopardy.

More worrying, however, is that a drive to achieve height without depth can cause serious long-term damage. If children were being asked to attempt physical outcomes in the way that they are being expected to achieve some mental ones, there would be a public outcry. The problem with damage to the learner is that it is not always as apparent as damage to the athlete. A young child expected to attempt a demanding and advanced gymnastic movement would fail. They would fail simply because their bodies are not sufficiently physically mature to cope with the demands on their muscles and skeletal frame. We would see that child fall – hurting bones, muscles, tendons and, perhaps worst of all, confidence and self-esteem. The result would be not only physical damage, but lasting emotional damage too. If only we could X-ray the mental and emotional damage caused by the unreasonable demands being made on many young children to perform mental tasks for which they are not developmentally ready.

Paradoxically, the drive to introduce educational experiences that are too formal too soon can endanger the very notion of achievement in the longer term. Many of us still believe that a significant part of this country's failure in getting children to write, in the prescribed way by the prescribed stage, is because they are being required to do so when they are just too young. While the rest of Europe continues to provide evidence that starting formal education at an older age enhances children's skills at a later stage (Mills and Mills 1998) we continue to bring children into unsuitable school environments earlier and earlier. The time is ripe for our government to acknowledge that the early learning experiences demonstrated in our nursery schools and combined centres (Sylva *et al.* 1999) are appropriate – and desirable – foundations for all children up to the age of 7.

Successful early learning is not necessarily about height at all. It is about laying foundations that are sufficiently broad and deep to support whatever heights each individual child wants to attain later on. The height of the final edifice should be the choice of the individual child. Our task, as early childhood educators, is to help each one lay the foundations to ensure that their individual potential can be realized.

Fact 3: The more stress a building is likely to face, the more flexible the foundations need to be

Current lives are increasingly stressful. For both adults and children there are pressures from revolutionary changes to lifestyles. The speed at which the world is changing demands a matching ability to learn faster; expectations of jobs for life have given way to worries about job insecurity and in today's fast-moving, high-tech world, skills need updating and people upskilling.

More than one author has referred to the disturbing statistics reported by the Child and Mental Health Services (CAMHS) that one in every five children suffers from mental health problems and that most children, however young, present with complex problems. What an indictment on our current society and how important that we address the causes of stress in children who are so young.

Stress, as we know, is often induced by situations over which we feel we have no control. For some children this stress stems from home situations that are unstable or threatening or where parents simply cannot cope with what life has brought their way. Other chapters have described the devastating effects of the negative cycle of underachievement, often brought about by the initial strains of poverty, the breakdown of family relationships, unemployment or abuse. In his book *Emotional Intelligence* (1996) Daniel Goleman describes how emotional distress can create deficits in a child's intellectual abilities, crippling their capacity to learn. If a child is stressed or fearful, if they anticipate failure or are made to feel stupid, then the flow of information they need to make responses to questions or problems in class can be inhibited and induce further failure.

Many of the children who arrive in our early childhood settings are living daily in the middle of emotional crisis. It is to be hoped that their educational experiences will be more positive and fulfilling, but all too often young children are finding themselves in an education system which is, in itself, stressful. The emphasis on testing and target setting, reduced opportunities for PE, creativity and play, all impinge on children's ability to be in control of the outcomes of their learning and place additional demands on their already fragile self-perceptions.

No other group of children so desperately needs the benefits of high-quality nursery education. The best educational foundations for children whose self-esteem is low and whose motivation is limited is a learning environment where there is choice over activities, resources and outcomes, where there are diverse opportunities to role play the preoccupations of real-life situations and where there are sensitive, approachable adults to support the possibly painful consequences. The Foundation Stage should give children endless opportunities to take the risks they want to take rather than being put in risky situations by adults, to solve problems because the problems are meaningful and relevant to them and because they care about the outcomes. Most of all, it should lead them to a realization that they can be independent and capable as learners and can take control over their learning and ultimately their lives.

Fact 4: When building on poor ground, the foundations must be strengthened to compensate

Children's very earliest learning is often rock-solid. From birth – and many would claim before birth – young children are learning in contexts that are relevant, meaningful and purposeful. Learning makes sense because it is driven by children's own desire to master the world around them. So by the time they come to school, most children have learnt skills, developed attitudes and arrived at understandings at a rate that will never again be repeated in their lives (Fisher 1996).

Children also bring with them to school a wealth of life experiences which may or may not have prepared them for the learning environment they will meet in an educational institution. For some children the world of school with its language, its instruction and its emphasis on books is an alien environment dictated by codes which are difficult to break (Willes 1983). It is the task of the early years practitioner to make educational experiences meaningful and relevant for all children. Educators need to know about the foundations for learning that every child has been laying since birth and then to support individuals to build on those foundations in ways that are appropriate to their earliest beginnings.

On a broader canvas, Chapters 4 and 7 describe the importance of recent government initiatives such as the Early Excellence Centres and Sure Start Projects which have been developed to meet the needs of children and their families and to support the concept that education is part of a network of important services which should help to enrich the life experiences of both children and the adults in their lives. Both initiatives recognize fully that parents and carers are children's primary and enduring educators and seek to work with and alongside these significant adults. Without their background knowledge and continued involvement and expertise, educators can only give each child the same educational diet of experiences and hope that it satisfies their learning appetites. In such circumstances some children will go hungry, some will not be able to digest all that is put on their plates, some will be made to feel sick and others consume things to which they are allergic or will develop a lifelong loathing. It is simply inadequate teaching to assume that all children can be given the same educational diet and find it equally satisfying and nutritious.

Every child has potential. Some educators have to work harder than others to ensure that this potential is realized in an educational setting. But the responsibility lies in the hands of practitioners working alongside families and communities to lay learning foundations that are appropriate for each individual child.

Fact 5: If new buildings are to be added to existing buildings, making the right connections between the foundations is crucial

Recent studies in brain development have highlighted to educators the importance of the connections which the brain makes in learning situations. More has been learnt about the brain in the last ten years than in all previous scientific history and, in particular, the incredible capacity of the brain has only recently been realized. Mercifully, it seems that it is not so much the number of brain cells but the number of connections that are made between those brain cells that determines how 'useful' a brain becomes (Greenfield 1997).

Science and technology have made it possible to *see* the growth of brain connections when a brain is stimulated and active and the devastating impact of diseases such as Alzheimers, when the brain becomes unable to make the simplest and most common connections ever again.

Young children's brains are relatively 'naked' in terms of the number of connections they have made, but the amazing feat of the developing brain is just how quickly these connections start to form. A crucial role of the early childhood educator is to help children in their attempts to make meaning in their worlds. So much is new, and so much is incomprehensible, and the connections between what is new and what has already been learnt will make secure some of the most important learning foundations for life.

Sometimes children put two and two together easily and make the right connections for themselves. Sometimes they repeat and repeat actions, relentlessly testing out new theories until they are satisfied that they understand how something is, or what happens when . . . At other times children's inexperience causes them to make wrong connections and – just like a jigsaw puzzle – these wrongly connected pieces can be the most difficult to dislodge. Children's current understandings, and misunderstandings, should be the guiding light for educators to plan future experiences and opportunities and to help children make successful connections between their new and existing knowledge.

The brain literally expands through use. Susan Greenfield is adamant that you 'use it or lose it' and that there are certain times in life when learning is at its zenith. Many of those critical periods are when children are young – especially around language development. This is not to get caught up in erroneous suggestions that after the age of 3 all worthwhile learning opportunities are somehow lost for ever (Bruer 2000). However, the incredible plasticity of the brain when children are young certainly means that this is the time when they are often at their most receptive, and deprivation – be it sensory or emotional – can have devastating consequences.

Fact 6: When testing foundations, early strength is not a reliable predictor of later strength

The educational experiences which children have in school are geared increasingly to the tests to which they are subjected. Cramming for tests at the end of Key Stage 1 has now become as much a part of the lives of some 7-year-olds as it once was for 15-year-olds. Those who predicted the negative impact of testing at age 7 have been proved, in many ways, to be right. Teachers report a narrowing of the curriculum and lost opportunities for creative, physical and more spontaneous learning. Parents tell of children in tears, bed wetting and not wanting to go to school. Children talk about 'being a nothing' when they predict they will not achieve Level 1 or 2 in the key stage tests.

Making judgements too early about what children can or have achieved can be dangerous and potentially damaging. It can negatively label a child, setting in motion a cycle of underachievement brought about by low expectations and self-fulfilling prophecies of poor ability. It leads to a 'can't do' culture, rather than to a celebration of what every young child can do and has achieved which, at this age and stage, should be recognized as truly remarkable.

Early testing can also narrowly define each child's achievements. Every child in this country is currently judged and labelled, at the age of 4, by their knowledge and skills in a specified range of aspects of literacy and numeracy and a jumbled collection of personal, social and emotional attributes. But, as has already been argued, the best foundations for learning are broad, rich and varied. A child may display talent in an aspect of the curriculum that this limited and limiting testing process discounts and which leads, in consequence, to such abilities being diminished in the eyes of practitioners, parents and, ultimately, the child.

Finally, early test results can be a false predictor of what a child might achieve later on. There is no divine rule that says achievement must be manifest by the age of 7. Indeed, as an early childhood educator I would claim that this is a dangerous premise. As suggested early in this chapter, a sound foundation to learning can mean that 'results' are not seen until a child is much older and some of the benefits of early education may take years to become apparent. That is why there is a particular danger in making judgements about ability too early. Who is to say that success at Key Stage 1 is an appropriate point at which to make a judgement about the efficacy of the early years curriculum? We should not forget that 10 years after pouring concrete, it is still getting stronger.

Making judgements about young children's ability, and their potential, on the basis of narrowly conceived tests is both inappropriate and potentially damaging. Early childhood educators need to know about the full range of what children currently know and can do in order to plan an appropriate curriculum that supports each child's future development. This should be achieved through a rigorous, ongoing process of assessment, based on first-hand observation of young children in action as learners, in contexts in which they are familiar and with peers and adults with whom they feel secure. Testing children too early leads to a premature narrowing of the curriculum and to erroneous judgements being made about children whose only 'failure' may be that they have simply not been alive for long enough.

Fact 7: If foundations are inadequate it is very, very expensive to underpin them later on

The recent high levels of investment in the early years is recognition of the growing body of evidence that if the foundation years of learning are inadequate then it is very expensive to effect remedial work later on. The excellent summary of the effects of early education on later development by Kathy Sylva for the RSA 'Start Right' report in 1994 concluded that, while the vast majority of research has shown that pre-school education leads to immediate, measurable gains in educational and social development, the most rigorous studies show that *high-quality* early education leads to lasting cognitive and social benefits in children which persists through adolescence and adulthood. The 'pay-off' much quoted from the High/Scope research is that for every $1 invested, a further $7 is saved later on in terms of economic savings to society. Now, in the initial evaluation of the Early Excellence Centres Pilot Programme in the UK (Bertram and Pascal 1999b), first findings show that for every £1 invested in Early Excellence Centre services for family support, £8 is saved on alternative services. I really like Gillian Pugh's analogy in the previous chapter that a fence at the top of the cliff is infinitely preferable to an ambulance at the bottom. There must be ongoing and extended investment in the earliest stages of life and learning if more complex and costly interventions are not to be necessary later on.

But when early interventions are right, it is more than money that is saved. In terms of the quality of life, those children who experienced the high-quality, active learning High/Scope programme were found, at age 27, to have significantly higher monthly earnings; significantly higher percentages of home ownership; significantly higher levels of schooling completed; significantly lower percentages receiving social services at some time in the previous 10 years and significantly fewer arrests (including significantly fewer arrests for crimes of drug making or dealing) (Schweinhart *et al.* 1993). As early childhood educators the foundation stage of experiences that we offer young children should help to give them the skills to manage later in their lives. High-quality early education should give children the 'extra pocket' talked about by educators from Reggio Emilia, from which children can draw throughout their lives at times when they need confidence, self-assurance and – in particular – resilience.

High-quality early education has its own foundations. A commitment to children's personal, social and emotional well-being and the skills of independence, problem solving, cooperation and collaboration are increasingly seen as life skills, necessary for everyone in whatever realm of life they may be. It is said that, in the future, employers will need people who are creative, adaptable, innovative, good at communicating and motivated (NACCCE 1999). Now where do we know there are learners like these? The people that society wants for tomorrow are in our nurseries today.

Conclusion

My architect colleague assures me that no one in his profession would ever erect a building without putting in the highest quality foundations, because the consequences would be too dire. Nor would anyone challenge the extensive amounts of time, money and expertise that are needed if it can be demonstrated that these resources are necessary for the job in hand. Finally, he was shocked at the thought that anyone without the professional skills to make such judgements would interfere with his professional recommendations about what constitutes quality. Let us hope that the introduction of the Foundation Stage – so carefully named by government ministers – will be a major step towards an acceptance by all concerned that the foundations of education should be every bit as professionally constructed as those for the foundations of buildings.

References

Achenbach, T. and Howell, C. (1989) Are America's children's problems getting worse? A 13 year comparison, *Journal of the American Academy of Child and Adolescent Psychiatry*, November.

Athey, C. (1990) *Extending Thought in Young Children*. London: Paul Chapman.

Audit Commission (1996) *Under-fives Count*. London: Bourne Press.

Audit Commission (1999) *Children in Mind: Child and Adolescent Services*. London: Audit Commission Publications.

Axline, V.M. (1964) *Dibs in Search of Self*. Harmondsworth: Penguin.

Ball, C. (1994) *Start Right: The Importance of Early Learning*. London: RSA.

Ball, M. (in press) *Intervening Early. How Primary Schools Help Young Children Get the Best from School*. London: DfEE.

Barber, M. (1996) *The Learning Game*. London: Victor Gollancz.

Bathurst, K. (1905) The need for national nurseries, *Nineteenth Century*, May: 818–27.

Bebbington, A. and Miles, J. (1989) The background of children who enter local authority care, *British Journal of Social Work*, 19: 349–68.

Bernstein, B. (1970) A critique of the concept of compensatory education, in D. Rubenstein and C. Stoneman, *Education for Democracy*. Harmondsworth: Penguin.

Berreuta-Clement, J.R. *et al.* (1984) *Changed Lives; The Effects of the Perry Pre-school Programme on Youth through Age 19*. Ypsilanti, MI: High Scope Press.

Bertram, A. and Pascal, C. (1999a) Accounting early for life long learning, in L. Abbott and H. Moylett (eds) *Shaping the Future: Early Education Reformed*. London: Falmer.

Bertram, A. and Pascal, C. (1999b) *Early Excellence Centres: First Findings.* London: DfEE.

Bertram, A. and Pascal, C. (2000) *The OECD Thematic Review of Early Childhood Education and Care: Background Report for the United Kingdom.* Worcester: University College Worcester, Centre for Research in Early Childhood.

Bertram, A.D. (1996) Effective early educators: a methodology for assessment and development. PhD Thesis, Coventry University.

Bilton, H. (1998) *Outdoor Play in the Early Years.* London: David Fulton Publishers.

Blacking, J. (1987) *A Common-sense View of All Music.* Cambridge: Cambridge University Press.

Blythman, J. (2000) *The Food our Children Eat.* London: Fourth Estate.

BPS (British Psychological Society) (2000) *ADHD: Guidelines and Principles for Successful Multi-agency Working.* London: BPS (Tel: 0116 254 9568).

Brazelton, T.B. (1992) *Heart Start: The Emotional Foundations of School Readiness.* Arlington, VA: National Center for Clinical Infant Programs.

Bronfenbrenner, U. (1974) *Is Early Intervention Effective? A Report on Longitudinal Evaluations of Preschool Programmes,* Vol. 2. Washington, DC: DHEW Office of Child Development.

Bruce, T. (1996) *Helping Young Children to Play.* London: Hodder and Stoughton.

Bruer, J. (1999) *The Myth of the First Three Years.* New York, NY: The Free Press.

Bruner, J. (1983a) *Child's Talk.* New York, NY: Norton.

Bruner, J. (1983b) *In Search of Mind: Essays in Autobiography.* New York, NY: HarperCollins.

Bruner, J. (1990) *Acts of Meaning.* Cambridge, MA: Harvard University Press.

Bruner J. (1996) *The Culture of Education.* London: Harvard University Press.

CACE (Central Advisory Council for Education) (England) (1967) *Children and their Primary Schools (The Plowden Report).* London: HMSO.

Carlsson-Paige, N. and Levin, D. (1990) *Who's Calling the Shots?* Gabriola Island, BC, Canada: New Society Publishers.

Carnegie Foundation (1994) *Starting Points: Meeting the Needs of our Youngest Children.* New York, NY: Carnegie Corporation.

Chomsky, N. (1957) *Syntactic Structures.* The Hague: Mouton.

Clanchy, J. (1998) I'm late! I'm late! I'm only three but I must achieve, *Independent,* 8 October.

Claxton, G. (1997) *Hare Brain Tortoise Mind.* London: Fourth Estate.

Coveney, P. (1967) *The Image of Childhood.* Harmondsworth: Penguin Books.

Cox, T. (ed.) (2000) *Combating Educational Disadvantage: Meeting the Needs of Vulnerable Children.* London: Falmer Press.

Cranston, M. (1983) *Jean-Jacques*. London: Allen Lane.

Dahaene, S. (1997) *The Number Sense*. London: Penguin Press.

David, T. (ed.) (1993) *Educating our Youngest Children: European Perspectives*. London: Paul Chapman.

David, T. (ed.) (1999) *Young Children Learning*. London: Paul Chapman.

Davie, R. *et al.* (1972) *From Birth to Seven*. London: Longman.

Davin, A. (1996) *Growing Up Poor: Home, School and Street in London 1870–1914*. London: Rivers Oram Press.

De Keller, L. (2001) How are children's cultural and emotional experiences represented in shared imaginative play? Unpublished research, Roehampton Institute, Froebel College.

DES (1990) *Starting with Quality* (The Rumbold Report). London: HMSO.

Department of Health (1995) *Child Protection: Messages from Research*. London: HMSO.

DfEE (1998) *The National Literacy Strategy*. London: DfEE.

DfEE (1999) *The National Numeracy Strategy*. London: DfEE.

DfEE (2000) *Guidance on the Organisation of the National Literacy Strategy in Reception Classes*. London: DfEE.

Donaldson, M. (1993) *Human Minds*. Harmondsworth: Penguin.

Donaldson, M., Grieve, R. and Pratt, C. (eds) (1983) *Early Childhood Development and Education*. Oxford: Basil Blackwell.

Dowling, M. (2000) *Young Children's Personal, Social and Emotional Development*. London: Paul Chapman Publishing.

Drummond, M.-J. (1996) Play, learning and the national curriculum: some possibilities, in T. Cox (ed.) *The National Curriculum and the Early Years*. London: Falmer Press.

Drummond, M.-J. (2000) Perceptions of play in a Steiner kindergarten, in L. Abbott and H. Moylett (eds) *Early Education Transformed*. London: Falmer Press.

Drury, R. (2000) Bilingual children in the pre-school years: different experiences of early learning, in R. Drury, L. Miller and R. Campbell, (eds) *Looking at Early Years Education and Care*. London: David Fulton Publishers.

Dunn, J. (1988) *The Beginnings of Social Understanding*. Cambridge, MA: Harvard University Press.

Dweck, C.S. and Leggett, E. (1988) A social-cognitive approach to motivation and personality, *Psychological Review*, 95(2): 256–73.

Edgington, M. (2000) My hopes and fears for early years, *Early Years Educator*, 2(1): 16–18.

Edwards, C., Gandini, L. and Foreman, G. (eds) (1995) *The Hundred Languages of Children*. New York, NY: Ablex Publishing.

Egan, K. (1991) *Primary Understanding: Education in Early Childhood*. London: Routledge.

Eisner, E. (1985) *The Art of Educational Evaluation: A Personal View*. Lewes: Falmer Press.

Elliott, E. and Dweck, C.S. (1988) Goals: an approach to motivation and achievement, *Journal of Personality and Social Psychology*, 54(1): 5–12.

EYCG (Early Years Curriculum Group) (1998) *Interpreting the National Curriculum at Key Stage 1*. Buckingham: Open University Press.

Fernald, A. (1993) Approval and disapproval: infant responsiveness to vocal affect in familiar and unfamiliar languages, *Child Development*, 64(3): 657–74.

Fisher, J. (1996) *Starting from the Child?* Buckingham: Open University Press.

Fisher, J. (1998) Fit for the purpose? A critique of the national framework for Baseline Assessment, *Education 3 to 13*, October: 9–14.

Fisher, J. (2000) The foundations of learning, *Early Education*, 31 Summer.

Freire, P. (1985) *Pedagogy of the Oppressed*. London: Pelican.

Fromm, E. (1951) *The Forgotten Language*. New York, NY: Grove Weidenfeld.

Furedi, F. (2001) *Paranoid Parenting*. Harmondsworth: Penguin Press.

Gardner, H. (1993) *Frames of Mind*, 2nd edition. London: Fontana Press.

Gardner, H. (1999) *Intelligence Reframed*. New York, NY: Basic Books.

Goleman, D. (1996) *Emotional Intelligence*. London: Bloomsbury Publishing.

Gopnik, A., Meltzoff, A. and Kuhl, P. (eds) (1999) *How Babies Think: The Science of Childhood*. London: Weidenfeld and Nicolson.

Gosden, P.H. (1969) *How They Were Taught*. London: Basil Blackwell.

Greenfield, S. (1997) *The Human Brain: A Guided Tour*. London: Weidenfeld and Nicolson.

Gregory, E. (ed.) (1997) *One Child, Many Worlds: Early Learning in Multicultural Communities*. London: David Fulton.

Handy, C. (1994) *The Empty Raincoat: Making Sense of the Future*. London: Hutchinson.

Hartley Brewer, E. (1999) *Hindered by Unhappiness: A Review of Primary School Interventions to Support Children who Cause Concern*. London: Coram Family.

Heyman, G., Dweck, C.S. and Cain, K. (1992) Young children's vulnerability to self blame and helplessness: relationship to beliefs about goodness, *Child Development*, 63: 401–15.

Hohmann, M., Barnet, B. and Weikart, D. (1979) *Young Children in Action: A Manual for Pre-schoolers*. Ypsilanti, MI: High Scope Educational Research Foundation.

Holdaway, D. (1979) *The Foundations of Literacy*. Gosford, NSW: Ashton Scholastic.

Holt, J. (1989) *Learning all the Time*. Ticknall, Derbyshire: Education Now.

House of Commons Education and Employment Select Committee (2000) *Early Years: Volume 1*. London: HMSO.

Howe, M. (1999) *Genius Explained*. Cambridge: Cambridge University Press.

Karmiloff-Smith, A. (1994) *Baby It's You!* London: Ebury Press.

Katz, L. (1995) *Talks with Teachers of Young Children*. Norwood, NJ: Ablex.

Katz, L. and Chard, S. (1989) *Engaging Children's Minds: The Project Approach*. Norwood, NJ: Ablex.

Kraemer, S. (1999) Promoting resilience: changing concepts of parenting and child care, *International Journal of Child and Family Welfare*, 3: 273–87.

Kumar, V. (1993) *Poverty and Inequality in the UK: The Effects on Children*. London: NCB.

Laevers, F. (1996) Social competence, self organisation and exploratory drive, and creativity: definition and assessment. Paper presented at the 6th European Early Childhood Education Research Association Conference on the Quality of Early Childhood Education, Lisbon, Portugal, September.

Laevers, F. and Van Santen, J. (1995) *Basic Book for an Experiential Preprimary Education*. Leuven Belgium: Centre for Experiential Education.

Lantieri, L. (1990) *The Resolving Conflict Creativity Problem 1989: Summary of Significant Findings of RCCP*. New Jersey, NJ: Metis Associates.

Lazar, I. and Darlington, R. (1982) The lasting effects of early education: a report from the Consortium for Longitudinal Studies, *Monographs of the Society for Research in Child Development*, 47: 2–3.

LeDoux, J. (1999) *The Emotional Brain*. London: Weidenfeld and Nicolson.

Lindon, J. (1999) *Too Safe for their Own Good?* London: National Early Years Network.

Lipman, M. (1989) *Philosophy Goes to School*. New Jersey, NJ: Temple University Press.

Little, M. and Mount, K. (1999) *Prevention and Early Intervention with Children in Need*. London: Ashgate.

Lorenz, C. (1946) *Studies in Animal and Human Behaviour*, Volume 1. Cambridge, MA: Harvard University Press.

Lowndes, G.A.N. (1960) *Margaret McMillan: The Children's Champion*. London: Museum Press.

MacBeath, J. (2000) Support for Lifelong Learning, in T. Cox (ed.) *Combating Educational Disadvantage*. London: Falmer Press.

Makins, V. (1997) *Not Just a Nursery: Multi-agency Early Years Centres in Action*. London: National Children's Bureau.

Malaguzzi, L. (1993) History, ideas and basic philosophy, in C. Edwards, L. Gardini and G. Forman (eds) *The Hundred Languages of Children*. Norwood, NJ: Ablex.

Mayall, B. (1990) Childcare and childhood, *Children and Society*, 4(4): 374–85.

Meek, M. (1985) Play and paradoxes: some considerations of imagination and language, in G. Wells and J. Nicholls, *Language and Learning: An Interactional Perspective*. London: Falmer Press.

Mental Health Foundation (1998) *Facts Not Fairy Tales: Mental Health and Illness in Children and Young People*, MHF Briefing No. 15. London: Mental Health Foundation.

Mental Health Foundation (1999) *Bright Futures*. London: Mental Health Foundation.

Mills, C. and Mills, D. (1998) *Britain's Early Years*. London: Channel 4 Television.

Mithen, S. (1996) *The Prehistory of the Mind*. London: Thames and Hudson.

Murphy, C. and Liu, M. (1998) Choices must be made, *Education 3 to 13*, 26(2): 13.

Nabuco, E. and Sylva, K. (1996) The effects of three early childhood curricula on children's progress at primary school. Paper to ISSBD conference, Quebec, Canada.

National Advisory Committee on Creative and Cultural Education (1999) *All Our Futures: Creativity, Culture and Education*. Sudbury: DfEE.

National Commission on Education (1993) *Learning to Succeed*. London: Heinemann.

New Zealand Ministry of Education (1996) *Te Whariki, Early Childhood Curriculum*. Wellington: Learning Media.

Ofsted (1993) *Access and Achievement in Urban Education*. London: HMSO.

Ofsted (2000) *Inspecting Subjects 3–11*. London: Ofsted.

O'Leary, J. (1999) Lessons at four put 'too much stress on pupils', *The Times*, 1 April: 5.

Oliver, C. and Smith, M. (2000) *The Effectiveness of Early Interventions*. London: Institute of Education.

Osborn, A.F. and Milbank, J.E. (1987) *The Effects of Early Education*. Oxford: Oxford University Press.

Paley, V.G. (1981) *Wally's Stories*. Harvard, MA: Harvard University Press.

Paley, V.G. (1988) *Bad Guy's Don't Have Birthdays*. Chicago, IL: University of Chicago Press.

Paley, V.G. (1991) *The Boy Who Would Be a Helicopter*. Harvard, MA: Harvard University Press.

Papousek, H. (1994) To the evolution of human musicality and musical education, in I. Deliege (ed.) *Proceedings of the 3rd International Conference on Music Perception and Cognition*. Liege, Belgium: ESCOM.

Penn, H. and Lloyd, E. (2001) *Report: The Potential for Partnership between Maintained Nursery Schools and the Voluntary and Community Early Years Sector*. London: UEL and the National Early Years Network.

Perkins, D. (1998) Learning for understanding. Paper presented to the West Lothian/Quality in Education Seminar, September.

Phillips, D. (1995) Giving voice to young children, *European Early Childhood Education Research Journal*, 3(2): 5–15.

Piachaud, D. and Sutherland, H. (2000) *How Effective is the British Government's Attempt to Reduce Child Poverty?* London: London School of Economics, University of London.

Piaget, J. (1952) *The Origins of Intelligence*. New York, NY: International Universities Press.

Pilling, D. (1991) *Escape from Disdavantage*. London: Falmer Press.

Plunkett, K. (1998) Connectionism and development, in M. Sabourin, F.I.M. Craik and M. Roberts (eds) *Advances in Psychological Science, Volume 2: Biological and Cognitive Aspects*. London: Psychology Press.

POST (Parliamentary Office of Science and Technology) (2000) *Report on Early Years Learning*. London: POST 140, Millbank.

Pound, L. (2000) Foundations or Formica. Paper prepared for BERA conference, Cardiff, September.

Pugh, G. (ed) (1996) *Contemporary Issues in the Early Years*, 2nd edn. London: NCB.

Pugh, G. (1999) Children and families: a view at the millennium, *Community Care*, September: i–viii.

Pugh, G., De'Ath, E. and Smith, C. (1994) *Confident Parents, Confident Children: Policy and Practice in Parent Education and Support*. London: National Children's Bureau.

QCA (Qualifications and Curriculum Authority) (QCA) (2000) *Curriculum Guidance for the Foundation Stage*. London: QCA/DfEE.

Ramachandran, V.S. and Blakeslee, S. (1999) *Phantoms in the Brain*. London: Fourth Estate.

Rees Jones, S. (2000) *Report: Developing and Extending Nursery School Services*. London: DfEE.

Resnick, L.B. (1987) *Education and Learning to Think*. Washington, DC: National Academy Press.

Roberts, R. (1996) *Self-esteem and Successful Early Learning*. London: Hodder and Stoughton.

Rogoff, B., Mistry, J., Goncu, A. and Mosier, C. (1993) Guided participation in cultural activity by toddlers and care givers, monographs of the Society for Research, *Child Development*, 58(8), Serial No. 236.

Rosenfeld, A. and Wise, N. (2000) *Hyper-parenting: Are You Hurting your Child by Trying too Hard?* New York, NY: St. Martin's Press.

Rowntree Foundation (2000) *Poverty and Social Exclusion in Britain*. York: Joseph Rowntree Foundation.

Rutter, M. (1985) Family and school influences on cognitive development, *Journal of Child Psychology* 26(5): 683–704.

Salovey, P. and Mayer, J. (1990) Emotional Intelligence, *Imagination, Cognition and Personality*, 9: 185–211.

SCAA (Schools Curriculum and Assessment Authority) (1997) *Baseline Assessment Scales*. London: SCAA.

Schweinhart, L., Weikart D., and Larner, M. (1986) Consequences of three pre-school curriculum models through age 15, *Early Childhood Research Quarterly* 1: 15–45.

Schweinhart, L.J., Barnes, H.V. and Weikart, D.P. (1993) *Significant Benefits: The High Scope Perry Pre-school Study through Age 27*. Ypsilanti, MI: High Scope Press.

Shore, R. (1997) *Rethinking the Brain*. New York, NY: Families and Work Institute.

Siegel, D. (1999) *The Developing Mind*. New York, NY: Guildford Press.

Sinclair, R., Hearn, B. and Pugh, G. (1997) *Preventive Work with Families: The Role of Mainstream Services*. London: National Children's Bureau.

Siraj-Blatchford, I. (1996) *The Early Years: Laying the Foundation for Racial Equity.* Stoke-on-Trent: Trentham Books.

Siraj-Blatchford, I. (2000) Early childhood pedagogy: practice, principles and research, in P. Mortimore (ed.) *Understanding Pedagogy and its Impact on Learning.* London: Paul Chapman.

Slavin, R.E., Karweit, N.L. and Wasik, B.A. (1994) *Preventing Early School Failure.* Needham Height, MA: Allyn and Bacon.

Steedman, C. (1990) *Childhood Culture and Class in Britain: Margaret McMillan (1860–1931).* London: Virago.

Storr, A. (1992) *Music and the Mind.* London: HarperCollins.

Sylva, K. (1994) The impact of early learning on children's later development, in *Start Right: The Importance of Early Learning.* London: Royal Society of Arts.

Sylva, K. (2000) Early childhood education to ensure a 'fair start for all', in T. Cox (ed.) *Combating Educational Disadvantage: Meeting the Needs of Vulnerable Children.* London: Falmer Press.

Sylva, K. and Evans, E. (1999) Preventing failure at school, *Children and Society*, 13(4): 278–86.

Sylva, K., Melhuish, E., Sammons, P. and Siraj-Blatchford, I. (1999) *Technical Paper 6A: Characteristics of Pre-School Environments: Report from the Effective Provision of Pre-School Education Research.* London: Institute of Education, University of London.

Sylva, K., Melhuish, E., Sammons, P. and Siraj-Blatchford, I. (2000) *The Effective Provision of Pre-school Education (EPPE) Project.* Briefing information prepared for the House of Commons Education Committee Enquiry into Early Years Education.

Sylva, K., Siraj-Blatchford, I. and Johnson, S. (1992) The impact of the UK national curriculum on pre-school practice: some 'top-down' processes at work, *OMEP International Journal of Education*, 24(1): 41–51.

Talay-Ongan, A. (1998) *Typical and Atypical Development in Early Childhood.* London: British Psychological Society.

Thomas, A. (1998) *Educating Children at Home.* London: Cassell.

Thomas, A. *et al.* (1989) Longitudinal study of negative emotional states and adjustments from early childhood through adolescence, *Child Development*, 54: 47–64.

Thomas, E. (2000) Strangled eggs and appydong, *Early Education*, 32, Autumn.

Tizard, B., Blatchford, P., Burke, J., Care, F., and Plewis, J. (1988) *Young Children in the Inner City.* Hove and London: Lawrence Erlbaum Associates.

Trevarthen, C. (1992) An infant's motives for thinking and speaking, in A.H. Wold (ed.) *The Dialogical Alternative.* Oxford: Oxford University Press.

Trevarthen, C. (1994) How children learn before school. Paper delivered at Newcastle University with the British Association for Early Childhood Education.

Trudell, P. (1994) *Education Review*, Autumn 1994, 8(2) (National Union of Teachers).

Unicef (2000) *Innocenti Report Card No. 1, June 2000. A League Table of Child Poverty in Rich Nations*. Florence, Italy: Innocenti Research Centre.

Van der Eyken, W. (1969) *The Pre-School Years*. Harmondsworth: Penguin Education Special.

Vygotsky, L.S. (1962) *Thoughts and Language*. Cambridge, MA: MIT Press.

Vygotsky, L.S. (1976) *Mind and Society*. Cambridge, MA: Harvard University Press.

Vygotsky, L.S. (1978) *Mind in Society: The Development of Higher Psychological Processes*. Cambridge, MA: Harvard University Press.

West, D. and Farrington, D. (1982) *Delinquency: Its Roots, Careers and Prospects*. London: Heinemann.

Whalley, M. (1996) *Learning To Be Strong*. London: Hodder and Stoughton.

Wigfall, V. and Moss, P. (in press) *More than the Sum of Its Parts? A study of a Multi-agency Childcare Network*. York: Rowntree Foundation.

Willes, M.J. (1983) *Children into Pupils*. London: Routledge and Kegan Paul.

Winters, S. (1998) International comparisons of student achievement, *Education 3 to 13*, 26(2): 26–32.

Woodhead, M. (1997) Psychology and the cultural construction of children's needs, in A. James and A. Prout, *Constructing and Reconstructing Childhood: Contemporary Issues in the Sociological Study of Childhood*. London: Falmer Press.

Index